MW01488259

Holt German Level 3

Komm mit!®

Activities for Communication

HOLT, RINEHART AND WINSTON
Harcourt Brace & Company
Austin • New York • Orlando • Atlanta • San Francisco • Boston • Dallas • Toronto • London

Contributing Writers

Patricia Callahan
Sharon Heller

Copyright © by Holt, Rinehart and Winston

All rights reserved. No part of this publication may be reproduced or transmitted in any form or by any means, electronic or mechanical, including photocopy, recording, or any information storage and retrieval system, without permission in writing from the publisher.

Teachers using KOMM MIT! may photocopy complete pages in sufficient quantities for classroom use only and not for resale.

Cover Photo/Illustration Credits
Background pattern: Copyright ©1992 by Dover Publications, Inc.
Group of students: George Winkler/HRW Photo; German sign: George Winkler/HRW Photo

KOMM MIT! is a registered trademark licensed to Holt, Rinehart and Winston.

Printed in the United States of America

ISBN 0-03-053998-6

1 2 3 4 5 6 7   066   03 02 01 00 99

Contents

Copyright © by Holt, Rinehart and Winston. All rights reserved.

SITUATION CARDS

Copyright © by Holt, Rinehart and Winston. All rights reserved.

To the Teacher

Oral communication is the most challenging language skill to develop and test. The **Komm mit!** *Activities for Communication* book helps students to develop their speaking skills and gives them opportunities to communicate in many different situations. The Communicative Activities and Situation Cards provide a variety of information-gap activities, role-playing scenarios, and interviews to assist students with the progression from closed-ended practice to more creative, open-ended use of German. The Realia reproduces authentic documents to provide students with additional reading practice using material written by and for native speakers. Included with the Realia are teaching suggestions and student activities showing how to integrate the four skills and culture into your realia lesson. With the focus on dialogue and real-life context, the activities in this book will help your students achieve the goal of genuine interaction.

Each chapter of *Activities for Communication* provides:

- **Communicative Activities** In each chapter two or four communicative, pair-work activities encourage students to use German in realistic conversation, in settings where they must seek and share information. The activities provide cooperative language practice and encourage students to take risks with language in a relaxed, uninhibiting, and enjoyable setting. The activities correspond to a particular **Stufe** and encourage use of functions, vocabulary, and grammar presented in that chapter section. Each activity may be used upon completion of the **Stufe** as a Performance Assessment, or may be recorded on audio or video tape for inclusion in students' portfolios. The activities may also be used as an informal review of the **Stufe** to provide additional oral practice.

- **Realia** Each chapter contains three reproducible pieces of realia that relate to the chapter theme and reflect life and culture in the German-speaking countries. Finding they can read and understand documents intended for native speakers gives students a feeling of accomplishment that encourages them to continue learning. The realia may be used to review the functions, vocabulary, and grammar presented in a particular **Stufe,** or may be used as additional practice at any point within a **Stufe.** Along with the blackline masters of the realia you will find suggestions for using the realia in the classroom. These suggestions include a combination of activities for individual, pair, and group work and focus on the skills of listening, speaking, reading, and writing, while at the same time exploring authentic cultural information.

- **Situation Cards** For each of the twelve chapters, three sets of interview questions and three situations for role-playing are provided in blackline master form. These cards are designed to stimulate conversation and to prepare students for speaking tests. The interviews or role-playing may be used as pair work with the entire class, as activities to begin the class period, as oral performance assessments upon completion of a **Stufe,** or to encourage oral practice at any point during study of a **Stufe.** These conversations may be recorded as audio or video additions to students' portfolios. Because the cards may be recycled throughout the scholastic year as review of chapters already completed, students will be rewarded as they realize they are meeting goals and improving their communicative abilities. To avoid having to copy the cards repeatedly, consider mounting them on cardboard and laminating them. They may be filed for use during the year as well as for future classes.

Copyright © by Holt, Rinehart and Winston. All rights reserved.

Communicative Activities

Name _____ Klasse _____ Datum _____

Communicative Activities 1-1A and 1-2A

1-1A You and your friend are planning a trip to Dresden. Each of you has gathered some information about several places to stay while visiting there. Exchange information with your friend and fill in the chart below. Then discuss with him or her where you should stay. Justify your choice.

	Wo?	Frühstück inklusiv?	Fernseher im Zimmer	Telefon im Zimmer	andere Vorteile	Preis pro Person
Hotel Marietta						
Pension	ganz zentral	nein	nein	nein	nein	DM 93,–
Jugend-herberge	in einem Vorort	kostet extra	im Fernseh-raum	nein	interessante Leute	DM 75,–
Gasthaus zur Semperoper						

Wir sollten im/in der _____ übernachten, weil_____

_____

_____

1-2A You are a customer planning your vacation at a travel agency in Berlin. You would like to spend between DM 2 000 and DM 2 500 on a **Pauschalreise** (*package trip*). You have four weeks of vacation and are trying to decide whether you want to spend most of your time in Germany or in another country. Tell your travel agent about your plans and your budget and then ask for suggestions. Take notes as your agent tells you about the various trips available, then tell the agent which travel options appeal to you most and why.

Notizen

_____

_____

_____

Welche Reise oder Reisen würdest du am liebsten machen? Warum?

_____

_____

Copyright © by Holt, Rinehart and Winston. All rights reserved.

COMMUNICATIVE ACTIVITIES

Communicative Activities 1-1B and 1-2B

1-1B You and your friend are planning a trip to Dresden. Each of you has gathered some information about several places to stay while visiting there. Exchange information with your friend and fill in the chart below. Then discuss with him or her where you should stay. Justify your choice.

	Wo?	Frühstück inklusiv?	Fernseher im Zimmer	Telefon im Zimmer	andere Vorteile	Preis pro Person
Hotel Marietta	15 Minuten mit dem Bus von der Stadtmitte	ja	ja	ja	Sauna	DM 170,–
Pension						
Jugend-herberge						
Gasthaus zur Semperoper	ganz zentral	ja	nein	nein	gemütlich, historisches Gebäude	DM 85,–

Wir sollten im/in der _____ übernachten, weil _____

_____

_____

1-2B You work at a Berlin travel agency. A client, your partner, needs your help in deciding what to do for vacation. Ask about his or her travel plans. Make sure you find out how much time and money he or she would like to spend on the vacation. Then make travel suggestions based on the following **Pauschalreisen** (*package trips*). Help your client decide what to do for his or her vacation.

PAUSCHALREISEN	

NORD AMERIKA:
  USA: Boston, New York, Washington D.C., Williamsburg
  8 Tage – DM 1209
  14 Tage – DM 2359
 	
  USA: Yellowstone, San Franzisko, Yosemite, Las Vegas, Grand Canyon, Los Angeles
  24 Tage – DM 2789
 	
  Karibik:
    Jamaika- *14 Tage* – DM 2059
    St. Croix- *7 Tage* – DM 1509
	AFRIKA:
	  Marokko: Tanger, Rabat, Casablanca, Marrakesch und andere historische Städte
	  14 Tage – DM 1432
	
	DEUTSCHLAND:
	  Frankfurt am Main: inklusive Karten für: Goethemuseum, Goethehaus, Konzert
	  5 Tage – DM 479
	
	  Hamburg: Karten für Les Misérables, Ausflüge zum Freibad in Wedel
	  7 Tage – DM 625

Copyright © by Holt, Rinehart and Winston. All rights reserved.

Communicative Activities 1-3A and 1-4A

1-3A Your German class is throwing a dinner party for some German exchange students. You and your partner have gathered information about the foods they like, dislike and cannot eat. Your partner has the information missing in your chart. Exchange information with your partner so that you can complete the chart. Then, ask some of your classmates what their eating preferences and restrictions are. Finally, with your partner, plan a menu for the dinner party. How does your menu compare to the menus of the other people in your class?

	besonders gern essen	nicht so gern essen	darf nicht essen
Sandra			
Petra			
Karl	Nudeln	Spinat	Schokolade
Heike			
Kurt	Pizza	Eier	nichts
Erich	Meeresfrüchte	Schweinefleisch	Erdnüsse
mein(e) Partner/in			
Ich			

Final menu: _____

_____

_____

1-4A You are the night nurse at the infirmary of a boarding school about to start your shift. Ask the nurse going off duty (your partner) about the patients currently in the infirmary so you can fill out your chart below. For example, what are their names? What's wrong with each of them? What special instructions did the doctor leave?

Name	Was ist los mit ihm/ihr?	Welche Medikamente/andere Merkmale?

Now imagine it's 6:00 AM at the end of your shift. Tell the nurse coming on duty what is wrong with each patient, and then give him or her an oral update on each patient.

Thomas M.
um 2 Uhr morgens
Aspirin genommen

Jürgen S.
schlecht geschlafen

Tanja K.
Fieber um Mitternacht: 39
hustet noch viel, hat
ziemlich viel Wasser getrunken

Ahmet O.
hat um 3 Uhr Medikament
gegen Schmerzen bekommen

Copyright © by Holt, Rinehart and Winston. All rights reserved.

COMMUNICATIVE ACTIVITIES

Communicative Activities 1-3B and 1-4B

1-3B Your German class is throwing a dinner party for some German exchange students. You and your partner have gathered information about the foods they like, dislike and cannot eat. Your partner has the information that is missing from your chart. Ask your partner for the information you need to complete the chart. Then, ask some of your classmates what their eating preferences and restrictions are. Finally, with your partner, decide on a menu for the dinner party. Compare your menu with the menus of the other people in the class.

	besonders gern essen	nicht so gern essen	darf nicht essen
Sandra	Gemüse	Meeresfrüchte	Erdbeeren
Petra	Fleisch/Wurst	Gemüse	nichts
Karl			
Heike	Salat	Fleisch	Schokolade
Kurt			
Erich			
mein(e) Partner/in			
Ich			

Final menu: _____

_____

_____

1-4B You are a nurse working the day shift at a boarding school infirmary. The evening nurse (your partner) is about to relieve you. You have written the following report of the afternoon's events. Answer the night nurse's questions based on the information in the report.

Thomas M.
Knöchel verstaucht
alle drei Stunden Aspirin
nehmen; muss sitzen bleiben
19.30 Uhr Aspirin genommen

Jürgen S.
Krabben gegessen
darauf allergisch reagiert
Magen- und Kopfschmerzen
braucht Ruhe, Flüssigkeit

Tanja K.
Grippe
Fieber: 38,9
Husten, Bauchschmerzen,
Kopfschmerzen; ruhig im
Bett bleiben, Flüssigkeit

Ahmet O.
das linke Bein gebrochen
den rechten Knöchel
verstaucht; muss ruhig im
Bett bleiben

Now imagine that you are the new nurse coming on duty. Your partner will explain what is wrong with each patient and give you an update on each one. Use this information to fill in the chart below.

Name	Was ist los mit ihm/ihr?	Welche Medikamente/andere Merkmale?

Komm mit! Level 3, Chapter 1

Copyright © by Holt, Rinehart and Winston. All rights reserved.

Communicative Activities 2-1A and 2-2A

2-1A You are an exchange student living in Berlin. You and a friend are planning a vacation for the upcoming spring holidays. You've both researched different places you would like to visit. Exchange information with your partner and use the information to fill in the chart below. After you have finished, discuss your travel plans with your partner. Then write a short paragraph about where you have decided to go on vacation and what you plan to do when you get there.

	Dresden	**München**	**Frankfurt**	**Bayrische Alpen**
Vorteile	historische Stadt, viele kulturelle Veranstaltungen		Goethehaus, Goethemuseum, übernachten bei meiner Schwester	
Nachteile	Luftverschmutzung, Jugendherberge in einem Vorort		ziemlich weit, von Berlin, schon die letzten Ferien da verbracht	
Rundfahrt	DM 145,00		DM 289,00	
Übernachtung	Jugendherberge, DM 10,00 pro Nacht		gratis bei meiner Schwester	

Wohin fahrt ihr? Warum dahin?

_____

_____

_____

2-2A You are a new student at school and have just joined the school's travel club. The next club meeting will be at your house and you need to buy the food and beverages for the meeting. Your partner has offered to help clean around your house while you shop. Discuss with your partner what you should buy, and where you should buy it. You will need to get directions to the store or stores you are going to. Then discuss with your partner what he or she should do at your house, and give him or her directions about what to do.

Was ich kaufen soll und wo: _____

_____

Wie ich zu den Läden komme: _____

_____

Was mein Partner oder meine Partnerin für mich machen wird: _____

_____

Copyright © by Holt, Rinehart and Winston. All rights reserved.

COMMUNICATIVE ACTIVITIES

 Communicative Activities 2-1B and 2-2B

2-1B You live in Berlin. You and a friend are planning a vacation for the upcoming spring holidays. Both you and your partner have researched different places to visit. Exchange information with your partner and fill in the chart below with the missing information. After you have shared all the information with your partner, discuss your travel plans together. Then, working with your partner, write a short paragraph about where you have decided to go on vacation.

	Dresden	München	Frankfurt	Bayrische Alpen
Vorteile		historisch, viele Museen, Alpen ganz nah		schöne Gegend, viel Natur, Ski laufen, wandern
Nachteile		ziemlich weit, teuer		zu ruhig vielleicht nicht genug Schnee
Rundfahrt		DM 327,00		DM 335,00
Übernachtung		Jugendherberge, DM 27,00 pro Nacht		Jugendherberge, DM 10,00

Wohin fahrt ihr? Warum dahin?

_____

_____

_____

2-2B The travel club from school is going to meet at your partner's house. You have offered to help by cleaning up while your partner does the last of the shopping for the snacks. Your partner is new to the area and doesn't know where to shop. First, take notes about what your partner should get and where. Also, fill in the chart below with the required information. Give your partner directions to the store or stores he or she needs to go to.

Was dein Partner oder deine Partnerin kaufen soll und wo: _____

_____

Wie er oder sie zu den Läden kommt: _____

_____

Wie ich ihm oder ihr helfen kann: _____

_____

Copyright © by Holt, Rinehart and Winston. All rights reserved.

Communicative Activities 2-3A and 2-4A

2-3A You and your partner are thinking about spending a weekend in Heidelberg. Both of you know a little bit about the city from different sources. Using the chart below, share the information you have with your partner. After you have finished, discuss with your partner whether you still want to go to Heidelberg and why or why not. Did you and your partner agree?

	Heidelberg	Woher ich das weiß
Wo?	am Neckar	in einem Buch gelesen
In welchem Bundesland?		
Sehenswürdig-keiten	altes Schloss, alte Universität, viele Amerikaner studieren an der Uni	Freund
Gegend	nicht weit vom Schwarzwald	gehört

2-4A You and your partner are planning a picnic for the upcoming weekend. Write down suggestions for where to go, what to bring, and how you will get there. Ask your partner what his or her suggestions are. Discuss the ideas (consider the weather) and decide together what to do.

	Wo?	Was bringen wir mit?	Wie kommen wir dahin?
Vorschläge:			
Die Vorschläge von meiner Partnerin oder meinem Partner:			
Wofür wir uns entscheiden:			

Copyright © by Holt, Rinehart and Winston. All rights reserved.

COMMUNICATIVE ACTIVITIES

 Communicative Activities 2-3B and 2-4B

2-3B You and your partner are considering spending a weekend in Heidelberg, Both of you know a little bit about the city from different sources. Using the chart below, share the information you have with your partner. After you have finished, discuss with your partner whether you still want to go to Heidelberg and why or why not. Did you and your partner agree?

	Heidelberg	**Woher ich das weiß**
Wo?		
In welchem Bundesland?	Baden-Württemberg	in einem Buch gelesen
Sehenswürdig-keiten	viele Konzerte, viele Ausländer an der Uni	Freund
Gegend	nicht sehr weit von Frankfurt	gehört

2-4B You and your partner are planning a picnic for the upcoming weekend. Write down suggestions for where to go, what to bring, and how you will get there. Ask your partner what his or her suggestions are. Discuss the ideas (consider the weather) and decide together what to do.

	Wo?	**Was bringen wir mit?**	**Wie kommen wir dahin?**
Vorschläge:			
Vorschläge von meiner Partnerin oder meinem Partner:			
Wofür wir uns entscheiden:			

Copyright © by Holt, Rinehart and Winston. All rights reserved.

Name _____ Klasse _____ Datum _____

3-1A At the request of the school psychologist, you have been asked to interview several classmates about what they do when they are feeling down: **Was machst du, wenn du dich mickrig fühlst?** Below is the information you got from four students. (Don't forget to include yourself in your survey!) Supply the answers to the questions the psychologist (your partner) asks about your data.

Jutta	Jens	Janos	Julia	Ich
sich schminken	Basketball spielen	lesen	radeln	
schwimmen gehen	neue Klamotten kaufen	Briefe schreiben	Musik hören	
ins Kino gehen	ins Tagebuch schreiben	joggen gehen	Hausaufgaben machen	
ihr Zimmer aufräumen	fernsehen	kochen	Klavier spielen	

3-2A You are a contestant on a television game show called *Guess the Celebrity!* Your partner is a celebrity guest. You have to guess who he or she is in order to win the prize, but you can only ask five questions related to appearance, personal characteristics, diet, and hobbies. Write some possible questions in the blanks below, and then ask your partner, the celebrity.

_____

_____

_____

_____

_____

_____

_____

Mein Partner oder meine Partnerin heißt

_____

Copyright © by Holt, Rinehart and Winston. All rights reserved.

COMMUNICATIVE ACTIVITIES

Communicative Activities 3-1B and 3-2B

3-1B You are the school psychologist and are working on a research project about what students do when they are feeling down. A student volunteer, your partner, has surveyed several classmates about the questions: **Was machst du, wenn du dich mickrig fühlst?** You are now on the phone with your partner. Get the information required below by asking such questions as: **Wie viele Schüler machen etwas, was mit dem Aussehen zu tun hat? Was machen sie?**

	Zahl	Aktivitäten
Aussehen		
Sport		
Hobbys		
Unterhaltung		
Pflichten		
Sonstiges		

3-2B Pretend you are a famous person who is making a special guest appearance on a television game show called *Guess the Celebrity!* A contestant, your partner, is going to try to guess who you are by asking questions. First, decide who you are going to be, and then make notes about your appearance, personal characteristics, diet and hobbies in the spaces provided below. Answer your partner's questions with as much detail as possible without giving away your identity.

Aussehen

_____

_____

_____

Eigenschaften

_____

_____

_____

Ernährung

_____

_____

_____

Hobbys

_____

_____

Komm mit! Level 3, Chapter 3

Copyright © by Holt, Rinehart and Winston. All rights reserved.

Communicative Activities 3-3A and 3-4A

3-3A You and your partner are the editors of an advice column for your student newspaper. You have a list of people who have recently written to you for help with their problems. Your partner has come up with a list of suggestions. Describe to your partner what is bothering each person on your list, and your partner will give you an appropriate suggestion. Next to each person's name, write the suggestion you both agree would be the best one.

Name	Problem
Tanja	bekommt schlechte Noten
Ahmet	fühlt sich mickrig
Maria	hat noch keine Sommerarbeit
Sven	hat mit den Eltern gestritten
Reinhold	hat mit seiner Freundin gestritten
Petra	hat eine Pechsträhne
Cordula	ist gestresst, weil sie zu viel zu tun hat
Rainer	muss ein bisschen abnehmen

3-4A You are a trainer at a local fitness club. You help clients by pairing them up with exercise buddies. A new client (your partner) is starting a fitness program and is looking for a compatible buddy. Listed below are brief profiles of other club members who are also looking for workout buddies. Help your partner select the best person by sharing what your other clients' exercise habits are.

STEFFEN Ich möchte ein bisschen abnehmen und fit werden. Deshalb habe ich vor, jeden Tag vor der Schule fünfundvierzig Minuten zu joggen. Ich werde auch Diät machen: das heißt, keine Süßigkeiten mehr essen, aber dafür mehr Obst und Gemüse essen.

LISBETH Ich möchte zunehmen. Ich werde dreimal in der Woche Bodybuilding machen, das heißt, dienstags und donnerstags nach der Schule, und jeden Samstagmorgen. Ich muss auch meine Ernährung ändern; ich esse von jetzt an drei Bananen pro Tag neben anderen Gerichten, und jedes Mal nach dem Bodybuilding werde ich ins Café gehen und ein Eis essen.

UTE Ich möchte einfach fitter werden. Im Moment kann ich kaum joggen oder schwimmen. Jedes Mal wenn ich versuche, Fußball zu spielen, bin ich immer nachher total geschafft. Deshalb werde ich anfangen, fünfmal in der Woche abends schwimmen zu gehen. Ich werde mit 15 Minuten Schwimmen anfangen. Nach einem Monat werde ich vielleicht schon eine Dreiviertelstunde schwimmen. Weil ich weder ab- noch zunehmen will, brauche ich keine Diät zu machen.

Copyright © by Holt, Rinehart and Winston. All rights reserved.

Communicative Activities 3-3B and 3-4B

3-3B You and your partner are editors of an advice column for the student newspaper. Your partner has a list of people and the issues that are bothering them. As your partner tells you what each person's problem is, look at your list of suggestions below, and pick one out that is appropriate for that person's problem. Make sure that your partner agrees that it is appropriate, then write the person's name next to the suggestion.

Name	Ratschlag
	Blumen schenken
	keine Süßigkeiten mehr essen
	fleißiger lernen
	mit den Eltern wieder gut sein
	in die Zeitung gucken
	positiver denken
	etwas für sich selbst tun
	Zeit nehmen, um zu relaxen

3-4B Imagine you have decided to join a fitness club. The club offers a special service that matches new members with a workout buddy. First, take notes about what you want to do to get or keep fit. What will you do? Do you need to lose weight? Gain weight? Will you go on a diet? What kind? What kind of exercises will you do? When? How often? Write down your plans in the space provided. Then with your partner, who works at the club, find out which members are looking for a workout buddy and decide who best matches your needs and why.

_____

_____

_____

_____

_____

_____

_____

_____

Der Partner für mich ist _____ , weil _____

_____

Copyright © by Holt, Rinehart and Winston. All rights reserved.

Communicative Activity 4-1A

a. You and a partner are working on a psychology project. Each of you has interviewed students for information on the topic "What do parents and children argue about?" Ask your partner how his or her interviewees responded to the question **Worüber gibt es zu Hause Streit?**, and share your information with your partner.

Rebecca	Robert	Regina	Rolf
ausgehen			Fernsehen
Geschirr spülen			Videospiele
Noten			laute Musik
			Hausaufgaben

b. The persons interviewed were asked: **Wie löst ihr Probleme zu Hause? Wie erreicht ihr mit den Eltern eine Lösung?** Based on the information in the chart above, who do you think is most likely to have made each of the following responses? Fill in your answers, then tell your partner what helped you make your decision.

_____ Wir streiten immer über dumme Kleinigkeiten bei mir zu Hause. Es ist bei mir ziemlich eng zu Hause; wir sind vier Kinder, meine Eltern und meine Großmutter. Wir kommen jeden Monat einmal zusammen, um die Hausarbeit unter allen aufzuteilen. Aber unser Plan geht normalerweise nach einer Woche oder so schief. Dann gibt es wiederum Streit.

_____ Na, zum Beispiel, meine Eltern haben immer gesagt, du bist noch ein Kind, du brauchst kein Geld. Es gab vorher immer Streit wegen Geld. Neulich haben wir einmal wirklich darüber diskutiert. Ich habe ihnen genau gesagt, wozu ich Geld brauche. Die hatten aber keine Geduld für meine Argumente. Leider bekomme ich immer noch kein Taschengeld, aber es gibt jetzt natürlich nicht so viel Krach darüber.

_____ Ob wir wirklich etwas gelöst haben, bezweifle ich. Meine Eltern haben mir genau gesagt, wann und wie ich alles machen muss. Zum Beispiel darf ich Rockmusik nur zwischen 14.00 und 20.00 Uhr hören. Davor oder danach darf ich nur klassische Musik anhören. Wenigstens mag ich klassische Musik wie Mozart und Haydn. Aber es nervt mich, dass meine Eltern nie nach meiner Meinung fragen. Sie sagen mir einfach, was ich machen darf und muss.

_____ Natürlich gibt es Missverständnisse zwischen mir und meinen Eltern. Es scheint mir immer, als ob nichts gelöst wird. Sie schimpfen ständig mit mir. Vorher hatte ich immer versucht, mich zu verteidigen, aber das geht natürlich nicht. Es führt dazu, dass sie nur ärgerlich auf mich werden, und mir verbieten, mit Freunden auszugehen. Jetzt vermeide ich Streit mit meinen Eltern. Was ich mache, ist ganz einfach. Ich höre ihnen nur ruhig zu, und alles, was sie sagen, bejahe ich. Dann gibt es wenigstens etwas Ruhe! Natürlich ändert es wirklich nichts, wenn man ganz einfach stumm zuhört, aber wenigstens gibt es etwas Ruhe. Man braucht auch etwas Ruhe zu Hause, oder?

Copyright © by Holt, Rinehart and Winston. All rights reserved.

COMMUNICATIVE ACTIVITIES

Communicative Activity 4-1B

a. You and your partner are working on a psychology project. You have interviewed students for information on the topic, "What do parents and children argue about?" Ask your partner how his or her interviewees responded to the question **Worüber gibt es zu Hause Streit?**, and share your information with your partner.

Rebecca	Robert	Regina	Rolf
	streiten mit den Geschwistern	Noten	
		Zimmer aufräumen	
	Geld	Wäsche waschen	
	Küchendienst	Geschirr spülen	

b. The informants were asked: **Wie löst ihr Probleme zu Hause? Wie kommt ihr mit den Eltern zu einer Lösung?** Based on the information in the chart above, who do you think is most likely to have made each of the following responses? Fill in your answers, then tell your partner what helped you make your decision.

_____ Wir streiten immer über dumme Kleinigkeiten bei mir zu Hause. Es ist bei mir ziemlich eng zu Hause; wir sind vier Kinder, meine Eltern und meine Großmutter. Wir kommen jeden Monat einmal zusammen, um die Hausarbeit unter allen aufzuteilen. Aber unser Plan geht normalerweise nach einer Woche oder so schief. Dann gibt es wiederum Streit.

_____ Na, zum Beispiel, meine Eltern haben immer gesagt, du bist noch ein Kind, du brauchst kein Geld. Es gab vorher immer Streit wegen Geld. Neulich haben wir einmal wirklich darüber diskutiert. Ich habe ihnen genau gesagt, wozu ich Geld brauche. Die hatten aber keine Geduld für meine Argumente. Leider bekomme ich immer noch kein Taschengeld, aber es gibt jetzt natürlich nicht so viel Krach darüber.

_____ Ob wir wirklich etwas gelöst haben, bezweifle ich. Meine Eltern haben mir genau gesagt, wann und wie ich alles machen muss. Zum Beispiel darf ich Rockmusik nur zwischen 14.00 und 20.00 Uhr hören. Davor oder danach darf ich nur klassische Musik anhören. Wenigstens mag ich klassische Musik wie Mozart und Haydn. Aber es nervt mich, dass meine Eltern nie nach meiner Meinung fragen. Sie sagen mir einfach, was ich machen darf und muss.

_____ Natürlich gibt es Missverständnisse zwischen mir und meinen Eltern. Es scheint mir immer, als ob nichts gelöst wird. Sie schimpfen ständig mit mir. Vorher hatte ich immer versucht, mich zu verteidigen, aber das geht natürlich nicht. Es führt dazu, dass sie nur ärgerlich auf mich werden, und mir verbieten, mit Freunden auszugehen. Jetzt vermeide ich Streit mit meinen Eltern. Was ich mache, ist ganz einfach. Ich höre ihnen nur ruhig zu, und alles, was sie sagen, bejahe ich. Dann gibt es wenigstens etwas Ruhe! Natürlich ändert es wirklich nichts, wenn man ganz einfach stumm zuhört, aber wenigstens gibt es etwas Ruhe. Man braucht auch etwas Ruhe zu Hause, oder?

Copyright © by Holt, Rinehart and Winston. All rights reserved.

C
O
M
M
U
N
I
C
A
T
I
V
E

A
C
T
I
V
I
T
I
E
S

Communicative Activity 4-2A

a. You and your partner are conducting a survey to find out how students get along with their parents. (**Wie kommst du mit deinen Eltern aus?**) You have collected part of the information and your partner has the rest. Exchange information and take notes in the blanks provided. Don't forget to include yourself and your partner in the survey.

ICH _____

_____

RENATE Meine Eltern sind eigentlich sehr nett zu mir. Wir sprechen oft über meine Probleme, und worum es geht. Sie wollen wissen, was mir wichtig ist, wer meine Freunde sind, usw. Sie geben mir ziemlich viel Freiheit, weil sie mir vertrauen.

MAX _____

_____

HASSAN Ich darf nichts von dem machen, was ich will, weil meine Eltern mich einfach nicht verstehen. Sie sind sehr streng und verbieten mir sogar, mit Freunden am Wochenende oder am Abend auszugehen. Ich habe oft mit ihnen darüber gestritten, aber das ändert nichts! Ich kann's kaum erwarten, bis ich 18 Jahre alt bin. Dann werde ich machen, was ich will!

ULI _____

_____

Mein Partner oder meine Partnerin: _____

_____

b. Now decide together if the students you surveyed would agree or disagree with the numbered statements below. Fill in the chart below with the required information.

1. Erwachsene versuchen nicht, Jugendliche zu verstehen.
2. Ich kann über alles mit meinen Eltern reden.
3. Kinder brauchen viele Regeln, denn es ist für sie besser.

Name	zustimmen	andere Meinung haben
ich		
Renate		
Max		
Hassan		
Uli		
Partner oder Partnerin		

Copyright © by Holt, Rinehart and Winston. All rights reserved.

Communicative Activity 4-2B

a. You and your partner are conducting a survey to find out how students get along with their parents. (**Wie kommst du mit deinen Eltern aus?**) You have collected part of the information and your partner has the rest. Exchange information and take notes in the blanks provided. Don't forget to include yourself and your partner in the survey.

ICH _____

_____

RENATE _____

_____

MAX Es gibt heutzutage viele Probleme für Jugendliche. Die Welt ist ziemlich gefährlich für uns. Wenn die Kinder das nicht verstehen, dann müssen uns die Eltern sagen, was wir machen dürfen und was nicht. Auch wenn die Kinder anderer Meinung sind, die Eltern wissen es besser als wir.

HASSAN _____

_____

ULI Ich kann über alles mit meinen Eltern diskutieren, aber das hilft selten. Sie sagen mir, wie ich mich benehmen soll, wann ich ausgehen darf, wann ich meine Hausaufgaben machen muss und so weiter. Sie hören gern meine Meinung, aber das ändert nichts. Sie können immer erklären, warum ich tun muss, was sie sagen.

Mein Partner oder meine Partnerin _____

_____

b. Now decide if the students you surveyed would agree or disagree with the numbered statements below. Fill in the chart below with the required information.

1. Erwachsene versuchen nicht, Jugendliche zu verstehen.
2. Ich kann über alles mit meinen Eltern reden.
3. Kinder brauchen viele Regeln, denn es ist für sie besser.

Name	zustimmen	andere Meinung haben
Ich		
Renate		
Max		
Hassan		
Uli		
Partner oder Partnerin		

Copyright © by Holt, Rinehart and Winston. All rights reserved.

COMMUNICATIVE ACTIVITIES

Communicative Activities 5-1A and 5-2A

5-1A You are visiting a friend in Germany whose mother and grandmother are talking about what they would do, if... Fill in the missing information in the chart below by asking your partner the appropriate questions. Then ask your partner what he or she would do, if... and answer your partner's questions.

Was würdest du machen, wenn ...

	du 12 wärst?	**du jetzt Zeit hättest?**	**es 2050 wäre?**
Großmutter			
Mutter	mit Jupp Schmitt tanzen	ins Kino gehen	einen Roman über das 20. Jahrhundert schreiben
Partner			
ich			

5-2A We interviewed several people on how they spent their time on the weekend, how they would rather have spent it, and why. Exchange information with a fellow interviewer by asking the questions in the table about his or her interviewee and then answering your partner's questions about your interviewee. Afterwards, you will interview each other with the same questions.

Ich heiße Jan Huxman, und ich bin 37 Jahre alt. Ich habe 3 Kinder, Alter 8, 6 und 3. Ich wollte am Wochenende die Garage aufräumen, aber es ging nicht. Weil mein achtjähriges Kind sich den Knöchel gebrochen hat, haben wir fast den ganzen Samstag im Krankenhaus verbracht. Am Sonntag musste ich Andreas, den 6jährigen, zu einer Geburtstagsfeier bringen. Obwohl so was den Kindern Spaß macht, wäre ich lieber mit ihnen zum Europapark gefahren. Dort hätten die Kinder gespielt bis zum Gehtnichtmehr, und ich hätte die neue Achterbahn fahren können. Ich hätte auch gern ein paar Briefe an Freunde geschrieben, aber da war keine Zeit mehr übrig.

	Interviewpartner/in des Partners	**Partner selbst**
Name		
Alter		
gemacht		
lieber gemacht		

Copyright © by Holt, Rinehart and Winston. All rights reserved.

Name _____ Klasse _____ Datum _____

Communicative Activities 5-1B and 5-2B

5-1B You are visiting a friend in Germany whose mother and grandmother are talking about what they would do, if... Fill in the missing information in the chart below by asking your partner the appropriate questions. Then ask your partner what he or she would do, if... and answer your partner's questions.

Was würdest du machen, wenn ...

	du 12 wärst?	**du jetzt Zeit hättest?**	**es 2050 wäre?**
Großmutter	ohne Schuhe angeln gehen	zur Uni gehen	zum Mond fliegen
Mutter			
Partner			
ich			

5-2B We interviewed several people on how they spent their time on the weekend, how they would rather have spent it, and why. Exchange information with a fellow interviewer by asking the questions in the table about his or her interviewee and then answering your partner's questions about your interviewee. Afterwards, you will interview each other with the same questions.

Ich heiße Felicia Brandt, und ich bin 17 Jahre alt. Am Sonntag musste ich zu Hause helfen. Ich durfte nicht ausgehen, weil meine Mutter sagte, dass mein Zimmer das reinste Chaos war. Also bin ich den ganzen Tag zu Hause geblieben und habe mein Zimmer aufgeräumt und sauber gemacht. Dann am Abend musste ich noch einige Hausaufgaben machen. Ich hätte lieber ferngesehen oder wäre lieber ins Kino gegangen, aber das ging nicht. Am Nachmittag hätte ich lieber mit unsrer Basketball-Mannschaft gespielt, die das Spiel auch gewann. Was ich eigentlich am liebsten gemacht hätte, wäre meine tolle Kusine in München besuchen. Nächstes Wochenende vielleicht.

	Interviewpartner/in des Partners	**Partner selbst**
Name		
Alter		
gemacht		
lieber gemacht		

Copyright © by Holt, Rinehart and Winston. All rights reserved.

Name _____ Klasse _____ Datum _____

5-3A You and your partner are the personal secretaries of various spontaneous jet-setters and contact each other to arrange appointments for your clients. In the first grid are the clients you need to make immediate appointments for, what they want to do, and with whom. The second grid lists your clients who are indisposed and why. Alternate setting up appointments for clients in the first grid.

BEISPIEL   DU **Heinz würde gern mit Annika Golf spielen.**
PARTNER **Es tut mir Leid, Annika ist gerade nach Berlin geflogen, um ihre Tante zu besuchen.**

deine Klienten	was machen?	mit wem?
Ute	die Rolle im Film üben	Felix
Erik	Tennis spielen	Meike
Udo	einkaufen gehen	Hans-Jürg
Lotte	reiten gehen	Marta

deine beschäftigten Klienten	was sie gerade machen
Dietmar	neuen Anzug kaufen
Axel	beim Graf *(count)* essen
Gabriele	schon in der Bibliothek sein
Lars	Offiziersschule besuchen

5-4A Es ist jetzt zwei Jahre her seit eurem Schulabschluss und du und dein(e) Partner(in) seht einander zum ersten Mal wieder. Berichte ihm oder ihr darüber, was eure Freunde vor dem Militär- oder Zivildienst machen wollten! Dein(e) Partner(in) sagt dir dann, was den Freunden nachher wirklich passiert ist. Als nächstes berichtet dein(e) Partner(in) über einige Freunde, und du kannst sagen, was ihnen passiert ist. Spielt dann die Situation vor!

vorher		nachher	
Berti und Heiner	Karl-Heinz	Frank	Gerd
wollen	*sollen*	*dürfen*	*müssen*
zuerst studieren	Panzer fahren lernen	Kinder betreuen	Gewehre reinigen

Situation: Du bist Deutsche(r) und gerade 18 geworden. In Deutschland gibt es jetzt die völlige Gleichberechtigung, und du musst jetzt den Militär- oder Zivildienst machen. Sag deinem Partner oder deiner Partnerin, was du jetzt machen willst, sollst, musst, etc!

Copyright © by Holt, Rinehart and Winston. All rights reserved.

Name _____ Klasse _____ Datum _____

 Communicative Activities 5-3B and 5-3B

5-3B You and your partner are the personal secretaries of various spontaneous jet-setters and contact each other to arrange appointments for your clients. In the first grid are the clients you need to make immediate appointments for, what they want to do, and with whom. The second grid lists your clients who are indisposed and why. Alternate setting up appointments for clients in the first grid.

BEISPIEL   DU **Heinz würde gern mit Annika Golf spielen.**
PARTNER **Es tut mir Leid, Annika ist gerade nach Berlin geflogen, um ihre Tante zu besuchen.**

deine Klienten	was machen?	mit wem?
Roswitha	Reise nach China buchen	Axel
Rainer	zum Poloplatz gehen	Lars
Rüdiger	zusammen zur Bibliothek gehen	Gabriele
Silvia	schnell zur Oma fliegen	Dietmar

deine beschäftigten Klienten	was sie gerade machen
Felix	Klavier üben
Hans-Jürg	mit der Prinzessin im Kino sein
Marta	den ganzen Tag schlafen
Meike	mit der Großtante einkaufen sein

5-4B Es ist jetzt zwei Jahre her seit eurem Schulabschluss und du und dein(e) Partner(in) seht einander zum ersten Mal wieder. Er oder sie berichtet dir darüber, was eure Freunde vor dem Militär- oder Zivildienst machen wollten! Sag ihm oder ihr, was den Freunden nachher wirklich passiert ist. Als nächstes sollst du auch über die Pläne einiger Freunde berichten, und dein(e) Partner(in) sagt dir, was ihnen passiert ist. Spielt dann die Situation vor!

nachher		vorher	
Berti und Heiner	Karl-Heinz	Frank	Gerd
müssen	*können*	*sollen*	*wollen*
zur Bundeswehr gehen	Offizier werden	im Krankenhaus arbeiten	die Straßen sauber machen

Situation: Du bist Deutsche(r) und gerade 18 geworden. In Deutschland gibt es jetzt die völlige Gleichberechtigung, und du musst jetzt den Militär- oder Zivildienst machen. Sag deinem Partner oder deiner Partnerin, was du jetzt machen willst, sollst, musst, etc!

Copyright © by Holt, Rinehart and Winston. All rights reserved.

COMMUNICATIVE ACTIVITIES

Communicative Activities 6-1A and 6-2A

6-1A Welche Medien mögen diese Personen am liebsten? Warum? Welche Medien mögen sie nicht? Warum nicht? Frag deine Partnerin oder deinen Partner!

	Mag	**Warum?**	**Mag nicht**	**Warum?**
Monika				
Michael	Fernsehen	schnell, leicht	Radio	kann nichts sehen
Michaela	Radio	man kann gleichzeitig was anderes tun	Zeitung	dauert zu lange, schwer zu lesen
Marcus				
Ich				
Mein Partner				

6-2A You and your partner have collected case studies of the television habits of German students. Read the following case study and provide your partner with the answers to his or her questions. Then fill in the chart below the case study by asking your partner the appropriate questions.

Ich heiße Andreas Schüler, und ich gehe aufs Reichenau Gymnasium in Leipzig. Ich bin 17 Jahre alt. Ich arbeite 15 Stunden in der Woche bei einer Computerfirma, wo ich Programmierungsassistent bin. Ich sehe bis 2 Stunden pro Tag fern—nicht mehr, weil ich zu wenig Zeit dafür habe. Ich sehe am liebsten Sendungen aus Amerika, Star Trek, Baywatch, und so weiter. Manchmal sehe ich die Nachrichten, und ich versuche, wenigstens immer ein paar Werbungen zu sehen. Ich finde es interessant, wie man die Reklame darstellt, weil ich eines Tages Reklame fürs Fernsehen schreiben und produzieren möchte. Ich sehe nur spätabends fern, wenn ich wirklich müde bin—zu müde, etwas anderes zu machen, und noch nicht müde genug, ins Bett zu gehen. Ich würde sagen, ich sehe fern, um mich zu entspannen.

	Schüler des Partners	**Mein Partner**	**Ich**
Name			
Alter			
Wie viel fernsehen?			
Warum?			
Lieblingssendungen			

Copyright © by Holt, Rinehart and Winston. All rights reserved.

COMMUNICATIVE ACTIVITIES

Communicative Activities 6-1B and 6-2B

6-1B Welche Medien mögen diese Personen am liebsten? Warum? Welche Medien mögen sie nicht? Warum nicht? Frag deine Partnerin oder deinen Partner!

	Mag	Warum?	Mag nicht	Warum?
Monika	Fernsehen	kann alles sehen	Zeitung	dauert zu lange, sich zu informieren
Michael				
Michaela				
Marcus	Zeitung	sich am besten informieren	Fernsehen	sensationell, wenig Auskunft
Ich				
Mein Partner				

6-2B You and your partner have collected case studies of the television habits of German students. Read the following case study and provide your partner with the answers to his or her questions. Then fill in the chart below the case study by asking your partner the appropriate questions.

Ich heiße Gisela Arnten, bin 18 Jahre alt und gehe aufs Reichenau Gymnasium in Leipzig. Während der Woche beschäftige ich mich ziemlich viel mit den Hausaufgaben und so, und ich arbeite nachmittags als Kellnerin in einem Café. Abends mache ich eine halbe Stunde Arbeitspause, um die Nachrichten im Fernsehen zu schauen. Ich interessiere mich sehr für Politik und Wirtschaft und möchte jeden Tag hören, was passiert ist. Ich würde gern die Zeitung lesen, weil man sich dadurch am besten informieren kann, aber dafür habe ich zu wenig Zeit. Ich schaue die Nachrichten im Fernsehen an, um wenigstens ein bisschen Information zu bekommen. Am Wochenende ist es anders; ich arbeite nicht, und man kann nicht den ganzen Tag mit den Hausaufgaben verbringen. Ich sehe am Wochenende viel mehr fern. Ich schaue mir, zum Beispiel, einen alten Film an, wenn es so was gibt. Ich mag auch die Sendungen, die mit Krankenhäusern zu tun haben. Ich würde sagen, samstags abends, wenn ich nicht ausgehe, sehe ich manchmal zwei, manchmal drei Stunden fern. Wenn ich wirklich k.o. bin und keine Energie habe, dann manchmal auch vier Stunden.

	Schüler des Partners	Mein Partner	Ich
Name			
Alter			
Wie viel fernsehen?			
Warum?			
Lieblingssendungen			

Copyright © by Holt, Rinehart and Winston. All rights reserved.

Communicative Activities 6-3A and 6-4A

6-3A Take turns with your partner asking him or her questions based on the cues below. Respond to his or her questions, saying that yours is the best, nicest, etc.

> BEISPIEL   DU **Hast du ein großes Haus?**
>   PARTNER **Ich habe das größte Haus!**

interessant/Buch/lesen

nett/Eltern/haben

informativ/Zeitungen/sein

gut/Noten/bekommen

groß/Poster von _____ /haben

6-4A Below are several opinions. Your partner has several others. Take turns with your partner following this procedure:
1. State the opinion given.
2. Your partner reacts to the given opinion with his or her personal opinion.
3. You react to your partner's opinion, agreeing or disagreeing.

Keine Zeitung ist so interessant wie die New York Times.

Keine Gemälde sind so avantgardistisch wie die Gemälde von Andy Warhol.

Keine Musik ist so laut wie die Musik von den Toten Hosen.

Keine Schule ist so groß wie unsere Schule.

Copyright © by Holt, Rinehart and Winston. All rights reserved.

COMMUNICATIVE ACTIVITIES

Communicative Activities 6-3A and 6-4A

6-3B Take turns with your partner asking him or her questions based on the cues below. Respond to his or her questions, saying that yours is the best, nicest, etc.

BEISPIEL   DU **Hast du ein großes Haus?**
             PARTNER **Ich habe das größte Haus!**

neu/Fernseher/haben

modern/Möbel/haben

alt/Großeltern/haben

intelligent/Klassensprecher(-in)/haben

viele/Kurse/besuchen

6-4B Below are several opinions. Your partner has several others. Take turns with your partner following this procedure:
1. State the opinion given.
2. Your partner reacts to the given opinion with his or her personal opinion.
3. You react to your partner's opinion, agreeing or disagreeing.

Keine Bücher sind so spannend wie die Bücher von Stephen King.

Keine Filme sind so lustig wie die Filme mit Dana Carvey.

Kein historisches Ereignis ist so wichtig wie der Fall der Berliner Mauer in Deutschland im

     Jahre 1989.

Keine Musik ist so schön wie die Musik von Händel.

Copyright © by Holt, Rinehart and Winston. All rights reserved.

Name _____ Klasse _____ Datum _____

7-1A You and your partner are working for an advertising company. You've conducted a survey, finding out what products people own, who remains faithful to one manufacturer, and which manufacturers seem to be more popular. Fill in the missing information in your chart by asking your partner: **Was für ein Fahrrad hat Steffan?**, etc. Then answer the questions below.

	Fahrrad	Fernsehapparat	CD	Computer
Steffan		Grundhaft	Sonya	
Ismar	Ralley			
Ilona	Nikishiki		Höhepunkt	ABC
Angela		Sonya	Grundhaft	

Schreib einen Bericht: Wer bleibt einem Hersteller treu? Welche Hersteller sind hier am meisten repräsentiert?

_____

_____

_____

7-2A Using **Stichwörter** *(key words)*, write your opinions about the following statements and jot down the basis for your opinions. Then ask your partner what his or her reactions are to the same statements and record these opinions. Remember, only use **Stichwörter**. After this is completed, answer the questions below.

	Meine Meinung	Grund	Meinung des Partners	Grund
1. Werbung manipuliert.				
2. Werbung stellt Frauen nur als Blickfang dar.				
3. Werbung informiert nicht.				
4. Den Lebensstil, den Werbung anpreist, kann man sich nicht leisten.				

Vergleich deine Meinungen mit denen deines Partners/deiner Partnerin! Stimmst du mit deinem Partner/deiner Partnerin überein? Oder meinst du, dass deine Meinungen „richtiger" sind? Warum?

_____

_____

_____

Copyright © by Holt, Rinehart and Winston. All rights reserved.

COMMUNICATIVE ACTIVITIES

Communicative Activities 7-1B and 7-2B

7-1B You and your partner are working for an advertising company. You've conducted a survey, finding out what products people own, who remains faithful to one
manufacturer, and which manufacturers seem to be more popular. Fill in the
missing information in your chart by asking your partner: **Was für ein Fahrrad
hat Steffan?**, etc. Then answer the questions below.

	Fahrrad	Fernsehapparat	CD	Computer
Steffan	Geschwind			ABC
Ismar		Sonya	Sonya	Sonya
Ilona		Höhepunkt		
Angela	Nikishiki			Nikishiki

Schreib einen Bericht: Wer bleibt einem Hersteller treu? Welche Hersteller sind hier am
meisten repräsentiert?

_____

_____

_____

7-2B Using **Stichwörter** *(key words)*, write your opinions about the following statements and jot down the basis for your opinions. Then ask your partner what
his or her reactions are to the same statements and record these opinions.
Remember, only use **Stichwörter**. After this is completed, answer the questions below.

	Meine Meinung	Grund	Meinung des Partners	Grund
1. Werbung manipuliert.				
2. Werbung stellt Frauen nur als Blickfang dar.				
3. Werbung informiert nicht.				
4. Den Lebensstil, den Werbung anpreist, kann man sich nicht leisten.				

Vergleich deine Meinungen mit denen deines Partners/deiner Partnerin!
Stimmst du mit deinem Partner/deiner Partnerin überein? Oder meinst du, dass
deine Meinungen „richtiger" sind? Warum?

_____

_____

_____

Copyright © by Holt, Rinehart and Winston. All rights reserved.

Communicative Activities 7-3A and 7-4A

7-3A Fill in the chart below by asking your partner questions like **Welche Werbung hat Johannes gesehen?**, etc. Then answer the questions below.

	Johannes	Nina	Thomas	Annika
Werbung	Spezi Cola		Frosta	
Beschreibung	2 Kinder spielen im Restaurant		Oma singt Oper in der Küche	
Reaktion	gefällt mir		ist mir angenehm	
Warum?	nicht seriös, witzig		erinnert mich an meine Oma	

Wie findest du diese Werbungen oder ähnliche, die du kennst? Wie reagierst du und warum?

_____

_____

_____

7-4A Nenn drei Werbungen, die dich nerven! Beschreib kurz die Werbungen in Stichwörtern und schreib, warum sie dich nerven! Beschreib dann deinem Partner oder deiner Partnerin die Werbungen und sag, warum sie dich nerven! Frag dann deine(n) Partner(in), welche Werbungen sie oder ihn nerven!

Ich

_____ _____ _____
_____ _____ _____
_____ _____ _____
_____ _____ _____

Partner/Partnerin

_____ _____ _____
_____ _____ _____
_____ _____ _____

Now ask your partner if he or she remembers your commercials, and what his or her reaction to them is. Does your partner agree with you, or does he or she have another opinion? Write a paragraph or two on these commercials, discussing whether you like or dislike the same kinds of commercials, and why.

Copyright © by Holt, Rinehart and Winston. All rights reserved.

COMMUNICATIVE ACTIVITIES

Communicative Activities 7-3B and 7-4B

7-3B Fill in the chart below by asking your partner questions like **Welche Werbung hat Johannes gesehen?**, etc. Then answer the questions below.

	Johannes	Nina	Thomas	Annika
Werbung		Postbank		Der General „Putzalles"
Beschreibung		Mann auf dem Mofa wirft einen Brief in den Kasten.		Frau putzt Küche
Reaktion		nervt mich echt		regt mich wirklich auf
Warum?		Schauspieler sieht sehr dumm aus!		stereotypische Rolle der Frau

Wie findest du diese Werbungen oder ähnliche, die du kennst? Wie reagierst du und warum?

_____

_____

_____

7-4B Nenn drei Werbungen, die dich nerven! Beschreib kurz die Werbungen in Stichwörtern und schreib, warum sie dich nerven! Beschreib dann deinem Partner oder deiner Partnerin die Werbungen und sag, warum sie dich nerven! Frag dann deine(n) Partner(in), welche Werbungen sie oder ihn nerven!

Ich

_____ _____ _____

_____ _____ _____

_____ _____ _____

_____ _____ _____

Partner/Partnerin

_____ _____ _____

_____ _____ _____

_____ _____ _____

Now ask your partner if he or she remembers your commercials, and what his or her reaction to them is. Does your partner agree with you, or does he or she have another opinion? Write a paragraph or two on these commercials, discussing whether you like or dislike the same kinds of commercials, and why.

Copyright © by Holt, Rinehart and Winston. All rights reserved.

Name _____ Klasse _____ Datum _____

8-1A Was für Vorurteile hatten diese Leute, bevor sie das andere Land kennen gelernt haben?

Name	Alter	Heimatland	Land besucht	frühere Meinung	jetzige Meinung
Joachim	17	Österreich	USA	alle Amerikaner kauen Kaugummi	manche Amerikaner kauen Kaugummi
Donna	16	USA	Deutschland	alle Deutschen sind ausländer-feindlich	Deutsche sind inte-ressant, intelligent und tolerant
Ich			Deutschland		
Mein(e) Partner(in)			Deutschland		

8-2A Think of any **Vorurteile** you had about Germans before you started studying German. Then ask your partner the following questions and answer your partner's questions. Record your partner's answers in **Stichwörtern** on another piece of paper. Then write an essay comparing his or her preconceptions with yours and discussing how they've changed.

Was für Vorurteile hattest du früher? Was hältst du jetzt von diesen Vorurteilen? Gibt es etwas, was dich bei den Deutschen überrascht hat? Warst du enttäuscht herauszufinden, dass die Deutschen deinen Vorstellungen nicht unbedingt entsprechen *(correspond to)*? **Erzähl ein wenig davon!**

Copyright © by Holt, Rinehart and Winston. All rights reserved.

COMMUNICATIVE ACTIVITIES

 Communicative Activities 8-1B and 8-2B

8-1B Was für Vorurteile hatten diese Leute, bevor sie das andere Land kennen gelernt haben?

Name	Alter	Heimatland	Land besucht	frühere Meinung	jetzige Meinung
Josh	17	Kanada	Deutschland	alle Deutschen fahren schnell auf der Autobahn	viele Deutsche fahren schnell auf der Autobahn
Maria	18	Deutschland	USA	Amerikaner sind naiv	viele Amerikaner haben etwas von der Welt gesehen
Ich			Deutschland		
Mein(e) Partner(in)			Deutschland		

8-2B Think of any **Vorurteile** you had about Germans before you started studying German. Then ask your partner the following questions and answer your partner's questions. Record your partner's answers in **Stichwörtern** on another piece of paper. Then write an essay comparing his or her preconceptions with yours and discussing how they've changed.

Was für Vorurteile hattest du früher? Was hältst du jetzt von diesen Vorurteilen? Gibt es etwas, was dich bei den Deutschen überrascht hat? Warst du enttäuscht herauszufinden, dass die Deutschen deinen Vorstellungen nicht unbedingt entsprechen (correspond to)? **Erzähl ein wenig davon!**

Copyright © by Holt, Rinehart and Winston. All rights reserved.

Communicative Activities 8-3A and 8-4A

8-3A You and your partner each have the comments of two people about their impressions before and after they spent time in a foreign country. Ask your partner the questions necessary in order for you to fill in the information below.

Name _____

Alter _____

Heimatland _____

Land besucht _____

frühere Meinung _____

_____

jetzige Meinung _____

_____

Ich heiße Josephine, bin 18 Jahre alt und komme aus Louisville, Kentucky. Ich habe letztes Jahr 8 Monate in Düsseldorf als Austauschstudentin verbracht. Ich war überrascht, denn ich hatte immer gedacht, dass die Deutschen ausländerfeindlich sind. Es stimmt aber nicht. Alle Deutschen, die ich kennen gelernt habe, waren offen und tolerant. Meine deutschen Freunde haben mir aber gesagt, dass es immer noch Leute gibt, die ausländerfeindlich sind. Diese Leute glauben nämlich, dass die Ausländer ihre Arbeitsplätze wegnehmen wollen. Aber die meisten Deutschen sind nicht so. Ich habe meine Meinung über die Deutschen geändert. Jetzt bin ich der Meinung, dass es in Deutschland so wie hier in Amerika einige Leute gibt, die ausländerfeindlich sind, aber dass die meisten Leute nichts gegen Ausländer haben.

8-4A Write down a list of some common stereotypes about Germans. Pretend your partner knows absolutely nothing about Germany but is about to spend a couple of months there. What suggestions, recommendations, and warnings could you offer to help make his or her trip smoother? Consider also the preconceptions and assumptions he or she may have about Germans.

_____

_____

_____

_____

_____

_____

Copyright © by Holt, Rinehart and Winston. All rights reserved.

COMMUNICATIVE ACTIVITIES

Communicative Activities 8-3B and 8-4B

8-3B You and your partner each have the comments of two people about their impressions before and after they spent time in a foreign country. Ask your partner the questions necessary in order for you to fill in the information below.

Name _____

Alter _____

Heimatland _____

Land besucht _____

frühere Meinung _____

_____

jetzige Meinung _____

_____

Ich heiße Arno, und ich komme aus Deutschland, aus München. Ich bin 18 Jahre alt. Als ich 17 war, habe ich mit meinen Eltern eine Reise durch die Vereinigten Staaten gemacht. Wir haben in New York ein Auto gemietet und haben New York, Washington D.C., Miami, Memphis, New Orleans, Dallas, Santa Fe, Las Vegas, Los Angeles und viele „National Parks" und kleinere Städte besucht. Ich hatte mir immer vorgestellt, dass die Amerikaner ein hektisches Leben führen, dass sie immer arbeiten, immer herumeilen, dass sie nie ruhen und nie spazieren gehen, um die Natur zu genießen. Das war alles falsch. Die Amerikaner, die ich kennen gelernt habe, waren entspannt und haben sich Zeit genommen, mich und meine Familie näher kennen zu lernen. In den „National Parks" haben wir viele Familien getroffen, die sich für die Natur interessieren und Vögel und andere Tiere gerne beobachten. Man sieht sie, wie sie mit dicken Büchern durch die Parks wandern und versuchen, die verschiedenen Vögel und sogar manchmal Pflanzen zu identifizieren. Das Leben der Amerikaner scheint mir doch nicht so hektisch zu sein!

8-4B Write down a list of some common stereotypes about Americans. Pretend your partner knows absolutely nothing about the United States, but is about to spend a couple of months there. What suggestions, recommendations, and warnings could you offer to help make his or her trip smoother? Consider also the preconceptions and assumptions he or she may have about Americans.

_____

_____

_____

_____

_____

Komm mit! Level 3, Chapter 8

Copyright © by Holt, Rinehart and Winston. All rights reserved.

Communicative Activities 9-1A and 9-2A

9-1A Worüber machen sie sich Sorgen?

Fill in the chart below by asking your partner appropriate questions. Then ask your partner for advice to give to the people who have concerns.

Name	Alter	Sorgen	Rat des Partners
Hamid	17	Ozonloch	
Andrea	18	Wasserverschmutzung	
Ich			
Mein(e) Partner(in)			

9-2A What does your partner suggest could or should be done about the following problems?

1. **Abgase von Autos**

_____

_____

_____

2. **UV-Strahlen**

_____

_____

_____

Copyright © by Holt, Rinehart and Winston. All rights reserved.

Name _____ Klasse _____ Datum _____

Communicative Activities 9-1B and 9-2B

9-1B Worüber machen sie sich Sorgen?

Fill in the chart below by asking your partner appropriate questions. Then ask your partner for advice to give to the people who have concerns.

Name	Alter	Sorgen	Rat des Partners
Silke	16	Müllberge	
Hanno	15	Abgase von Autos	
Ich			
Mein(e) Partner(in)			

9-2B What does your partner suggest could or should be done about the following problems?

1. **Waldsterben**

_____

_____

_____

2. **Der häufige Gebrauch von Einwegflaschen**

_____

_____

_____

34 Activities for Communication

Komm mit! Level 3, Chapter 9

Copyright © by Holt, Rinehart and Winston. All rights reserved.

Communicative Activities 9-3A and 9-4A

9-3A Read the following statement a German student made about the environment. Your partner is reading a similar statement. Ask your partner what the student is doing for the environment now. Then find out what he or she would have done for the environment in the past, had he or she known what needed to be done. Fill in the missing information below by asking your partner the appropriate questions.

Name _____

Alter _____

früher _____

_____

jetzt _____

_____

Ich heiße Irma, bin 17 Jahre alt und wohne in Ostberlin, also in der ehemaligen DDR. Ich mache jetzt so viel wie möglich für die Umwelt, aber früher war es anders. Wenn ich davon gewusst hätte, hätte ich nicht so viel Wasser verschwendet. Ich hätte die leeren Dosen zum Container gebracht. Ich hätte Getränke, wie jetzt, in Mehrwegflaschen gekauft und die Flaschen immer zu den Geschäften zurückgebracht.

9-4A If the following situations were reality, what would your partner do for the environment?

Dein Partner ist deutscher Kanzler.

_____

_____

_____

Dein Partner hat viel Zeit.

_____

_____

_____

Copyright © by Holt, Rinehart and Winston. All rights reserved.

Communicative Activities 9-3B and 9-4B

9-3B Read the following statement a German student made about the environment. Your partner is reading a similar statement. Ask your partner what the student is doing for the environment now. Then find out what he or she would have done for the environment in the past, had he or she known what needed to be done. Fill in the missing information below by asking your partner the appropriate questions.

Name _____

Alter _____

früher _____

_____

jetzt _____

_____

Ich heiße Ingo und wohne in Lübeck, das ist in Schleswig-Holstein. Ich bin jetzt 18 und bin für die Umwelt sehr aktiv. Es war aber nicht immer so. Ich wusste nämlich nicht, was ich alles tun könnte, um der Umwelt nicht zu schaden. Wenn ich mehr davon gewusst hätte, hätte ich Altpapier gesammelt und es wieder verwerten lassen. Ich hätte alte Batterien nie in den Müll geworfen, und ich hätte den Müll sortiert und zum Container gebracht, so wie ich das jetzt seit 5 Jahren tue.

9-4B If the following situations were reality, what would your partner do for the environment?

Dein Partner ist sehr reich.

_____

_____

_____

Dein Partner kennt viele Leute, die ihren Mitmenschen helfen wollen.

_____

_____

_____

Copyright © by Holt, Rinehart and Winston. All rights reserved.

Communicative Activities 10-1A and 10-2A

10-1A Was würden diese Leute tun, wenn sie mehr Zeit für kulturelle Interessen hätten?
Ask your partner the appropriate questions to fill in the missing information.

Name	Alter	Stadt	hauptsächlich	eventuell
Roswitha	28	Dresden	ins Kino gehen	alle Filme von Fassbinder sehen
Lothar	48	Leipzig	ins Theater gehen	Musicals wie „Cats" ansehen
Udo				
Christa	19	Halle	ins Konzert gehen	regelmäßig Konzerte von Bands wie „U2" und „die Toten Hosen" besuchen
Ebba				
Axel				
Ich				
Mein(e) Partner(in)				

10-2A Was ist wichtig? Was ist weniger wichtig?
You and your partner both have statements from German students. Find out which cultural events or activities are important to the students, which are less important, which they couldn't imagine doing without, and which cultural figures they envy and admire. Ask your partner the appropriate questions to find out the information below.

Name _____ Alter _____

wichtig _____

warum? _____

weniger wichtig _____

warum? _____

nicht vorstellen können _____

beneiden _____

bewundern _____

Ich heiße Handan und bin 18 Jahre alt. Ich wohne in Berlin, aber ich komme aus der Türkei. Ich finde, dass Kunst eine große Rolle im Leben spielt. Weniger wichtig für mich sind Musik und Theater, weil sie flüchtig sind, also bloß einen kurzen Moment dauern. Aber bei einer Kunstausstellung kann man so lange vor einem Kunststück stehen bleiben, wie man will. Ich mag besonders gern Bildhauer so wie, zum Beispiel, Ernst Barlach. Ich kann mir ein Leben ohne Bildhauerkunst nicht vorstellen. Ich will einmal Bildhauerin werden. Ich bewundere die Werke von Michelangelo, weil sie so naturgetreu sind. Und ich beneide meine Freundin Silke, weil sie besser zeichnen kann als ich. Ich weiß noch nicht, ob ich gut bildhauern kann, weil ich es noch nie probiert habe. Ich muss noch eine Weile warten, bis ich in der Ausbildung bin.

Copyright © by Holt, Rinehart and Winston. All rights reserved.

COMMUNICATIVE ACTIVITIES

 Communicative Activities 10-1B and 10-2B

10-1B Was würden diese Leute tun, wenn sie mehr Zeit für kulturelle Interessen hätten?
Ask your partner the appropriate questions to fill in the missing information.

Name	Alter	Stadt	hauptsächlich	eventuell
Roswitha				
Lothar				
Udo	15	Rostock	ins Theater gehen	ins Sonntagskonzert gehen
Christa				
Ebba	18	Meißen	ins Konzert gehen	ins Kammertheater gehen
Axel	26	Weimar	in die Stadtbibliotek gehen	Gedichte von Goethe lesen
Ich				
Mein(e) Partner(in)				

10-2B Was ist wichtig? Was ist weniger wichtig?
You and your partner both have statements from German students. Find out
which cultural events or activities are important to the students, which are less
important, which they couldn't imagine doing without, and which cultural figures
they envy and admire. Ask your partner the appropriate questions to find out the
information below.

Name _____ Alter _____

wichtig _____

warum? _____

weniger wichtig _____

warum? _____

nicht vorstellen können _____

beneiden _____

bewundern _____

Ich heiße Uwe und bin 17 Jahre alt. Was für mich keine so große Rolle spielt, ist Kunst, also die
bildende Kunst. Was für mich dagegen sehr wichtig ist, ist Musik. Ich mag Musik deswegen so
gerne, weil ich nicht so gut sehen kann: ich bin nämlich halb blind. Mir gefallen alle Arten von
Musik, aber besonders klassische Musik. Ich mag aber Pop und Rock auch sehr gerne. Ich
bewundere Annie Lennox, nicht nur weil sie ein Popstar ist, sondern auch, weil sie eine klassische Ausbildung hat. Sie hat Oper studiert, habe ich gehört. Ich selber kann kaum singen, aber
ich spiele ganz gut Gitarre. Wenn ich nur besser singen könnte, würde ich auch ein Popstar
werden. Ich beneide Leute wie Bob Dylan, Neil Young und Tracy Chapman, die sowohl singen
als auch Gitarre spielen können. Ich könnte mir ein Leben ohne meine Gitarre nicht vorstellen.
Es macht mir unheimlich viel Spaß, Musik zu hören, aber Musik zu machen, macht mir sogar
mehr Spaß; ich kann mir nichts Besseres vorstellen!

Copyright © by Holt, Rinehart and Winston. All rights reserved.

Name _____ Klasse _____ Datum _____

10-3A Ihr seid Reporter für die Schülerzeitung und besucht ein Konzert. Während der Pause interviewt ihr einige Leute. Wofür interessieren sie sich? Warum? Teile deine Information deinem Partner oder deiner Partnerin mit, und schreibe seine oder ihre Information auf! Am Ende könnt ihr euch selbst interviewen.

Name	Alter	Stadt	kulturelle Interessen	Warum?
Simone	17	Schwerin	Oper	die Kostüme so schön finden
Rainer	19	Magdeburg	Filme	die Handlung spannend sein
Konrad	15	Potsdam	Kunstausstellungen	moderne Kunst mögen
Erika				
Volker				
Lotte				
Ich				
Mein(e) Partner(in)				

10-4A You and your partner both have descriptions of a part of the same person's evening at the theater. Make a list of everything that happened at the theater in your partner's description by asking the appropriate questions.

Was wurde alles gemacht?

_____

_____

_____

_____

_____

Wir sind ins Theater gekommen, und wir haben dem Platzanweiser unsere Eintrittskarten gezeigt. Er hat uns dann auf unsere Plätze gebracht. Die Musiker sind auf die Bühne gekommen und haben ein bisschen geübt. Dann haben sie ihre Instrumente gestimmt. Die Dirigentin ist dann auf die Bühne gekommen, und wir haben alle geklatscht. Dann hat das Orchester die Erste Symphonie von Brahms gespielt.

Komm mit! Level 3, Chapter 10   Activities for Communication **39**

Copyright © by Holt, Rinehart and Winston. All rights reserved.

COMMUNICATIVE ACTIVITIES

 Communicative Activities 10-3B and 10-4B

10-3B Ihr seid Reporter für die Schülerzeitung und besucht ein Konzert. Während der Pause interviewt ihr einige Leute. Wofür interessieren sie sich? Warum? Teile deine Information deinem Partner oder deiner Partnerin mit, und schreibe seine oder ihre Information auf! Am Ende könnt ihr euch selbst interviewen.

Name	Alter	Stadt	kulturelle Interessen	Warum?
Simone				
Rainer				
Konrad				
Erika	13	Eisenach	Orchester Konzerte	Posaune laut spielen
Volker	20	Stralsund	Bücher	gern tolle Geschichten lesen
Lotte	18	Erfurt	Ballet	gern tanzen
Ich				
Mein(e) Partner(in)				

10-4B You and your partner both have descriptions of a part of the same person's evening at the theater. Make a list of everything that happened at the theater in your partner's description by asking the appropriate questions.

Was wurde alles gemacht?

_____

_____

_____

_____

_____

Während der Pause sind wir ein bisschen herumgelaufen, und wir haben etwas getrunken und gegessen. Ich habe eine Freundin getroffen, und wir haben ein bisschen geplaudert. Nach der Pause hat das Orchester die Akademische Ouvertüre von Brahms gespielt und noch ein paar Stücke, aber ich bin leider dabei eingeschlafen. Ich bin aufgewacht, als die Zuhörer plötzlich viel und laut geklatscht haben. Nach dem Konzert sind wir ins Café gegangen, wo wir wieder mal gegessen und getrunken haben. Dann sind wir nach Hause gegangen.

Copyright © by Holt, Rinehart and Winston. All rights reserved.

Name _____ Klasse _____ Datum _____

11-1A Welche Pläne dieser Leute stehen schon fest?

Ask your partner what plans for the future the people listed below have already made. Ask for each person's information and report to your partner using a different expression each time.

Sylvia	
Jürgen	eine Lehre als Friseur machen
Jochen	
Theresa	Kauffrau werden
Mein(e) Partner(in)	

11-2A Worauf legen diese Schüler/diese Leute großen Wert?

Ask your partner what these people find important and why. There are many different ways to express what is important. Try to think of a different way to express what is important every time you ask or report.

Name	wichtig	Warum?
Steffi	viel Geld	Sicherheit haben
Heiko	Kinder	viel von Kindern lernen
Eberhard		
Antje		
Mein(e) Partner(in)		

Copyright © by Holt, Rinehart and Winston. All rights reserved.

Name _____ Klasse _____ Datum _____

COMMUNICATIVE ACTIVITIES

Communicative Activities 11-1B and 11-2B

11-1B **Welche Pläne dieser Leute stehen schon fest?**

Ask your partner what plans for the future the people listed below have already made. Ask for each person's information and report to your partner using a different expression each time.

Sylvia	an der Uni Politologie studieren
Jürgen	
Jochen	eine Ausbildung als Betriebsmechaniker machen
Theresa	
Mein(e) Partner(in)	

11-2B **Worauf legen diese Schüler/diese Leute großen Wert?**

Ask your partner what these people find important and why. There are many different ways to express what is important. Try to think of a different way to express what is important every time you ask or report.

Name	wichtig	Warum?
Steffi		
Heiko		
Eberhard	interessante Arbeit	sonst ist es langweilig
Antje	Kunst	man kann sich ausdrücken
Mein(e) Partner(in)		

42 Activities for Communication

Komm mit! Level 3, Chapter 11

Copyright © by Holt, Rinehart and Winston. All rights reserved.

Communicative Activities 11-3A and 11-4A

11-3A Was haben sie für die Zukunft vor?

Share with your partner the following information and he or she will provide you with information to fill in the chart.

Name	Zukunftspläne	Warum?
Frau und Herr Schmitt	ein Haus auf dem Land kaufen	Ruhe vom Stadtlärm
Lydia	heiraten, 3 Kinder haben	immer viele Leute um sich haben
Johannes		
Frau und Herr Tappe		
Die Eltern meines Partners		
Mein Partner		

11-4A Was werden sie mit 30 Jahren alles gemacht haben? Frag deinen Partner oder deine Partnerin und mach dir Notizen!

Name: _____

Alter: _____

Was er/sie alles mit 30 gemacht haben wird:

Ausbildung: _____

Beruf: _____

_____

Familie: _____

_____

Ich heiße Heiko und bin 18 Jahre alt. Nächstes Jahr werde ich das Abitur machen, und dann gehe ich an die Uni. Dort will ich Englisch und Sprachwissenschaft studieren, weil ich Professor werden will. Wenn ich 30 bin, werde ich schon eine Stelle als Professor bekommen haben, vielleicht sogar in England oder in Nordamerika. Ich werde noch keine Familie haben, weil ich mit dreißig immer noch unabhängig sein will. Vielleicht werde ich mit vierzig verheiratet sein und ein oder zwei Kinder haben.

Copyright © by Holt, Rinehart and Winston. All rights reserved.

Communicative Activities 11-3B and 11-4B

11-3B **Was haben sie für die Zukunft vor?**
Share with your partner the following information and he or she will provide you with information to fill in the chart.

Name	Zukunftspläne	Warum?
Frau und Herr Schmitt		
Lydia		
Johannes	Jura studieren, Anwalt werden	viel Geld und Autos
Frau und Herr Tappe	Geld sparen	eine Reise um die Welt
Die Eltern meines Partners		
Mein Partner		

11-4B Was werden sie mit 30 Jahren alles gemacht haben? Frag deinen Partner oder deine Partnerin und mach dir Notizen!

Name: _____

Alter: _____

Was er/sie alles mit 30 gemacht haben wird:

Ausbildung: _____

Beruf: _____

_____

Familie: _____

_____

Ich bin die Hanna, und ich bin 15 Jahre alt. Ich interessiere mich jetzt für so viele Sachen, dass es schwierig ist zu sagen, was ich alles mit 30 getan haben werde. Ich glaube, dass ich Weltraumfahrerin werden könnte, wenn ich an die Uni gehe und Physik und Chemie studiere. Mit dreißig möchte ich schon einmal auf dem Mars herumgelaufen sein. Und ich hoffe, dass ich schon verheiratet sein werde. Ich möchte aber erst später Kinder haben, vielleicht mit fünfunddreißig oder so.

Copyright © by Holt, Rinehart and Winston. All rights reserved.

Name _____ Klasse _____ Datum _____

12-1A Welche Probleme haben diese Leute? Was würde dein(e) Partner(in) ihnen empfehlen? Warum?

Ask your partner what the problems of the people listed below are, then ask him or her what advice he or she would give them and why.

Name	Problem	Rat des Partners	Warum?
Silke	kein Geld, den Führerschein zu machen		
Franz			
Hans-Jörg			
Irma	interessiert sich nicht für die Schule; bekommt schlechte Noten		

12-2A Welche Berufe haben diese Personen? Was ist die Meinung deiner Partnerin oder deines Partners zu diesen Berufen? Würde er oder sie auch mal so einen Beruf ausüben wollen? Warum?

Name	Alter	Beruf	Meinung des Partners	Warum?
Herr Ruf	48	Musiklehrer		
Frau Becker	32	Bankkauffrau		
Robert				
Sylvia	25	Industriemechanikerin		
Frau Dorn				
Herr Scholler				

Copyright © by Holt, Rinehart and Winston. All rights reserved.

COMMUNICATIVE ACTIVITIES

Communicative Activities 12-1B and 12-2B

12-1B Welche Probleme haben diese Leute? Was würde dein(e) Partner(in) ihnen empfehlen? Warum?

Ask your partner what the problems of the people listed below are, then ask him or her what advice he or she would give them and why.

Name	Problem	Rat des Partners	Warum?
Silke			
Franz	braucht neue Klamotten; Familie gibt kein Geld dafür		
Hans-Jörg	so beschäftigt mit der Schule; keine Zeit für Freunde		
Irma			

12-2B Welche Berufe haben diese Personen? Was ist die Meinung deiner Partnerin oder deines Partners zu diesen Berufen? Würde er oder sie auch mal so einen Beruf ausüben wollen? Warum?

Name	Alter	Beruf	Meinung des Partners	Warum?
Herr Ruf				
Frau Becker				
Robert	27	Kinderarzt		
Sylvia				
Frau Dorn	39	Bibliothekarin		
Herr Scholler	57	Deutschprofessor		

Copyright © by Holt, Rinehart and Winston. All rights reserved.

Name _____ Klasse _____ Datum _____

12-3A Bin ich dein Traumpartner?

As editor of a singles magazine you have to share information with a fellow editor on personal ads the magazine has received. After you secure the information on the characteristics of these clients, share your own with the other editor.

Name	Aussehen	Beruf	Interessen
Konrad	klein, schlank	Lehrer	Sport
Sebastian			
Petra			
Sara			
Michael	groß, blond	Künstler	Geschichte
Tanja	groß, rote Haare	Musikerin	Hausmusik
dein Partner			

12-4A Was wollen diese Studenten werden? Wie können sie das machen?

Find out what these students want to do for a living, and ask your partner for advice on how they might best achieve their professional goals.

Name	zukünftiger Beruf	Rat des Partners
Andreas	Soziologieprofessor	
Beate	Sportlehrerin	
Christine	Musikerin/Violinistin	
Dieter		
Elke		
Felix		

Copyright © by Holt, Rinehart and Winston. All rights reserved.

Name _____ Klasse _____ Datum _____

12-3B Bin ich dein Traumpartner?

As editor of a singles magazine you have to share information with a fellow editor on personal ads the magazine has received. After you secure the information on the characteristics of these clients, share your own with the other editor.

Name	Aussehen	Beruf	Interessen
Konrad			
Sebastian	dunkel, langes Haar	Student	Film, Literatur
Petra	graue Augen	Friseuse	Punkmusik
Sara	schöne Hände	Ärztin	Ballet, Tanzen
Michael			
Tanja			
dein Partner			

12-4B Was wollen diese Studenten werden? Wie können sie das machen?

Find out what these students want to do for a living, and ask your partner for advice on how they might best achieve their professional goals.

Name	zukünftiger Beruf	Partners Rat
Andreas		
Beate		
Christine		
Dieter	Schauspieler	
Elke	Weltraumfahrerin	
Felix	Zahnarzt	

Copyright © by Holt, Rinehart and Winston. All rights reserved.

Realia

COMMUNICATIVE ACTIVITIES

TREFF-sicheren Ferienspaß erleben; die spontane Wochenendreise oder den schon längst geplanten Kurzurlaub genießen. In zentraler Lage und reizvoller Landschaft. TREFF HOTELS bieten Ihnen in Deutschland und der Schweiz zukünftig über 50x ideale Voraussetzungen für erholsamen Urlaub *und* erfolgreiche Veranstaltungen. Wo Sie uns brauchen, für erlebnisreiche Ferien oder produktive Tagungsergebnisse: **anrufen!** Wir informieren, organisieren und reservieren.

Große Allee 1-3 • 34454 Arolsen
Telefax (05691) 89 04 30

Advertisement, "…wo Sie uns brauchen!," from *Focus*. Reprinted by permission of **Treff Hotels AG, Arolsen, Germany.**

Copyright © by Holt, Rinehart and Winston. All rights reserved.

COMMUNICATIVE ACTIVITIES

Realia 1-2

Empfehlung der Woche

Israel.
Scharon-
Früchte
Stück
0.⁷⁹

bei uns nur
1.⁵⁹
Spanischer Endiviensalat
Kl. II. Stück

Spanischer Paprika
mix, Kl. II, 500 g-Netz
1.⁹⁷

Jungbullenfleisch aus Bayern

bei uns nur
11.⁹⁹

Rinderrouladen- oder Schmorbraten
aus der Keule, 1 kg

Rinderfilet
*besonders zart, am Stück
oder in Scheiben, 1 kg*
38.⁹⁹

Rindersteak natur
*mit Pfeffer oder
Kräuterbutter, 1 kg*
17.⁹⁹

bei uns nur
16.⁹⁹

Rindersteakfleisch
aus den besten Stücken der Keule, 1 kg

Langer Einkaufsabend - jeden Donnerstag bis 20.30 Uhr geöffnet
(Unsere Märkte in Nieder-Mörlen und Wetzlar sind nur bis 20.00 Uhr geöffnet.)

Darmstadt Rheinstr. 99 ☎ 0 61 51 / 8 63 95 • **Da.-Weiterstadt** Robert-Koch-Str. 1 ☎ 0 61 51 / 8 62 51-2 • **Dietzenbach** Offenbacher Str. ☎ 0 60 74 / 20 31-3 • **Diez** Am Backsteinbrand 6 ☎ 0 64 32 / 6 20 46 • **Dudenhofen** Nieder-Rodener Str. ☎ 0 61 06 / 20 45 • **Egelsbach** K.-Schumacher-Ring 4 ☎ 0 61 03 / 4 30 91 • **Frankfurt Bergen-Enkheim** Im Hessencenter, Borsigalle ☎ 0 61 09 / 38 36 • **Frankfurt-Griesheim** Lärchenstraße 110 ☎ 0 69 / 38 82 00-08-09 • **Frankfurt Nordwest-Zentrum** Nidacorso 24 ☎ 0 69 57 40 64-6 • **Friedrichsdorf** Im Dammwald 5 ☎ 0 61 72 / 73 80 • **Gießen** Schiffenberger Weg ☎ 06 41/ 79 20 15 • **Griesheim/Da.** Flughafenstr. 7 ☎ 0 61 55 / 6 10 68 • **Hanau** Grimm-Center, F. -Ebert-Anlage 2 ☎ 0 61 81 / 25 60 48 • **Heppenheim** Tiergartenstraße ☎ 0 62 52 / 7 20 81 • **Herborn** Hinterthal 2-4 T ☎ 0 27-72 / 5 20 41-4 • **Heusenstamm** Werner-von-Siemens-Str. ☎ 0 61 04 / 50 89 • **Karben** 1 Am Warthweg / B3 ☎ 0 60 39 / 70 16 • **Michelstadt** W.-Rathenau-Allee 24 ☎ 0 60 61 / 6 01-3 • **Neu-Isenburg** im Isenburg-Zentrum ☎ 0 61 02 / 3 30 93 • **Nieder-Mörlen** Kettelerstr. ☎ 0 60 32 / 8 20 42 • **Raunheim** Liebfrauenstr. ☎ 0 61 42 / 4 40 51-2 • **Rodenbach** 1 Am Aueweg T ☎ 0 61 84 / 5 00 41-3 • **Steinheim** Pfaffenbrunnenstr. 124 ☎ 0 61 81 / 6 20 31 • **Taunusstein-Hahn** Kleiststraße ☎ 0 61 28 / 30 56 • **Wetzlar-Steindorf** Alte Straße ☎ 0 64 41 / 2 30 84

Copyright © by Holt, Rinehart and Winston. All rights reserved.

Name _____ Klasse _____ Datum _____

Realia 1-3

COMMUNICATIVE ACTIVITIES

Deutsches Buchstabieralphabet

A = Anton
Ä = Ärger
B = Berta
C = Cäsar
Ch = Charlotte
D = Dora
E = Emil
F = Friedrich
G = Gustav
H = Heinrich
I = Ida
J = Julius
K = Kaufmann
L = Ludwig
M = Martha
N = Nordpol
O = Otto
Ö = Ökonom
P = Paula
Q = Quelle
R = Richard
S = Siegfried
Sch = Schule
T = Theodor
U = Ulrich
Ü = Übermut
V = Viktor
W = Wilhelm
X = Xanthippe
Y = Ypsilon
Z = Zacharias

Internationales Buchstabieralphabet
(die großgeschriebenen Buchstaben werden betont)

A = Alpha   AL-fa
B = Bravo   BRA-wo
C = Charlie   TSCHA-li
D = Delta   DELL-ta
E = Echo   EK-o
F = Foxtrott   FOKS-trott
G = Golf   GOLF
H = Hotel   ho-TELL
I = India   IN-dia
J = Juliett   DSCHU-li-ETT
K = Kilo   KI-lo
L = Lima   LI-ma
M = Mike   MAIK
N = November   no-WEM-ber
O = Oskar   OSS-kar
P = Papa   PAPA
Q = Quebec   KWE-beck
R = Romeo   RO-mio
S = Sierra   si-ERR-a
T = Tango   TAN-go
U = Uniform   JU-niform
V = Victor   WIK-tor
W = Whisky   WISS-ki
X = Xray   EKS-re
Y = Yankee   DSCHÄN-ki
Z = Zulu   ZU-lu

Übertragung von Zahlen
(mit deutscher und englischer Aussprache; die großgeschriebenen Buchstaben werden betont)

0 = Null = ZERO
1 = Eins = OAN
2 = Zwo = TUU
3 = Drei = TRIE
4 = Vier = FO-er
5 = Fünnef = FA-if
6 = Sex = SIX
7 = Sieben = SEW-en
8 = Acht = EHT
9 = Neun = NAIN
Komma = Komma = DE-simel

Komm mit! Level 3, Chapter 1   Activities for Communication   **53**

Copyright © by Holt, Rinehart and Winston. All rights reserved.

Using Realia 1-1, 1-2, 1-3

Realia 1-1: Treff Hotels ad

1. **Reading (Slower Pace)** Ask students to skim the ad first for meaning, picking out familiar words and phrases. Then have them read it through carefully, identifying the words they know by underlining them. You may want them to use a specific color for each type of word. Verbs may be underlined in red, nouns in blue, adjectives in green, adverbs in orange, conjunctions with a black arrow or bridge shape, etc. Also, have them list on a separate sheet of paper all the vocabulary they don't know. Were the students able to discern much of the meaning from context clues and illustrations? Allow the whole class to volunteer information about the ad until they have uncovered as much information as possible. You may want to compile a class list of new vocabulary by asking each student to write on the board or on a transparency one word that he or she did not recognize. Each student writes only words that have not yet been listed. Do this until all the unknown words have been listed. Go over the vocabulary with the class and then read the ad again. Can they make more sense of it now?

2. **Writing** You may want to have students write their own ads using the new vocabulary. Address individual visual and tactile learner needs by having students illustrate the ad or by using pictures from magazines to cut and paste. You may want them to play the role of ad designers. They can make up their own logos and company names.

3. **Speaking** Tell students that they are going on an imaginary extended class trip through Germany. They will be staying in various cities located on the map in the ad. You may want to create an enlarged copy of the ad or have another map of Germany prominently displayed for this activity. Have students work in pairs. Each pair plans an itinerary and then role-plays in front of the class a situation in which one student calls hotels in the various cities to make reservations and the other is the desk clerk giving information about rates, room availability, and accommodations. If you wish to add an extra challenge, have the caller ask about special activities, historical landmarks, and cultural highlights of particular cities.

4. **Thinking Critically** Have students tell you the difference between the factual information contained in the ad and the promotional claims. What distinguishes each?

Realia 1-2: TOOM MARKT ad

1. **Listening** Describe a particular food item to the students and tell them a price. Ask the students if the price is accurate or inaccurate.

2. **Reading** Ask students several questions about the prices of different food items pictured and have students find the answers in the text. You might ask them to identify the address and phone number of three or four market locations. This can be an oral or written activity.

3. **Group Work/Role-playing** In this scenario a parent is asking a teenage son or daughter to go shopping for a dinner party the parent is giving the next day. Different groups may be assigned different situations. In one situation, for example, the youth has been given a certain amount of money and a list of items to buy. The money isn't enough to cover the costs. Ask the group to create a short skit dealing with this situation. The skit should involve the parent, the child, and

Copyright © by Holt, Rinehart and Winston. All rights reserved.

the store clerk. In a second situation, the food must be prepared that evening and it's already after 6:00 PM. How would the group handle that? A third situation might have the parent and son or daughter shopping together in the market. The mother requests that the child ask the store clerk for specific information about certain items. Perhaps what the parent wants is not immediately available. You may also consider allowing students to create their own situations.

4. **Writing** Bring in or have students bring in market ads from the daily newspaper. Each student writes a brief description of his or her typical diet for a week. (This may be a description or a list depending upon ability level.) **Math link:** Ask each student to calculate an estimated cost for his or her weekly food consumption.

5. **Thinking Critically** Based on the above activity, ask students to compare expensive diets to less expensive ones. For a greater challenge, you may want students to determine the best possible diet for the least amount of money.

6. **Writing (Challenge)** Have students choose one food item and write as much about it as possible. For instance, grapefruit is obviously a fruit. It belongs to the citrus family. It is grown on trees, in orchards, in warm climates. The rind is generally yellow but sometimes is also red or pink. The fruit is usually either yellow or pinkish-red. The fruit is naturally divided into sections. The grapefruit is round and is usually larger than a fist, about five inches in diameter. It is high in Vitamin C and fiber, etc. Challenge the students to say as much as possible about the food item of their choice.

Realia 1-3: Deutsches Buchstabieralphabet

1. **Thinking Critically** Have your students compare and contrast the German alphabet to the English alphabet. Explain that people taking purchase orders over the phone and telephone operators often use the alphabet code given here to ensure correct spelling of names and addresses. You may want to ask your students to find out if there is a standardized code used in English, and, if so, what it is. (Hint: What language is used for the **Internationales Buchstabieralphabet**? Ask students to think about why most of the words are English-based.)

2. **Speaking/Spelling** Have students work in pairs. They should take turns spelling aloud target vocabulary, using the **Deutsches Buchstabieralphabet** and figuring out what the word is. The listener can tell the speaker if the word was spelled correctly or incorrectly. You may wish to provide students with German/English dictionaries with which to check the accuracy of their work.

3. **Writing/Reading** Ask students to use the **Deutsches Buchstabieralphabet** as if it were a secret code. Ask them to write a brief message using the code. You may want to suggest a minimum or maximum number of sentences. Put the messages on slips of paper or index cards and then have students exchange messages and decode them by rewriting the message in normal spelling. If you wish, students may respond to the messages received.

4. **Speaking** Have students role-play a situation in which one person is lost in a German city and cannot find the person he or she is trying to locate. The other person is an operator helping him or her. (Explain that this alphabet is in actual use in Germany. If they were to call a German telephone operator, he or she would ask for the name of the person in question. Tell them they should not be surprised if, for example, in repeating the name **Schmidt**, the operator said, „**Siegfried, Cäsar, Heinrich, Martha, Ida, Dora, Theodor.**" The operator is not listing or asking for first names!)

Copyright © by Holt, Rinehart and Winston. All rights reserved.

Name _____ Klasse _____ Datum _____

 Realia 2-1

Globetrotter buchen über International Booking Network

Wer die Welt sehen und viel erleben, seine Reisekasse aber schonen möchte, wird das "International Booking Network" (IBN) der Internationalen Jugendherbergsföderation zu schätzen wissen. IBN bietet den Vorteil einer umgehenden Reservierung in Jugendherbergen auf der ganzen Welt—mit umgehender schriftlicher Bestätigung. Das Deutsche Jugendherbergswerk beteiligt sich daran. DJH-Mitglieder können in den angeschlossenen Jugendherbergen *Übernachtungsplätze* (teilweise bis zu sechs Nächten) im voraus reservieren. IBN— eine sichere Sache.

Zur Zeit können Sie im Jugendgästehaus Düsseldorf und in der Jugendherberge München über IBN buchen. Wir sind bestrebt, weitere Jugendherbergen einzubeziehen. Ferner bieten wir diesen Service auch über die DJH-Hauptgeschäftsstelle in Detmold an. Sie brauchen nur den markierten

Abschnitt auszufüllen. Wir wählen uns für Sie in das internationale Telefonnetzwerk ein und reservieren die gewünschten Übernachtungen. Sie erhalten einen Gutschein, den Sie bei Ihrer Ankunft in der Jugendherberge vorlegen. Die Bezahlung erfolgt in DM, dabei fallen keine Geldumtauschgebühren an. Die Preise sind abhängig von Ihrem Alter, dem Standard des Hauses, den eingeschlossenen Leistungen (z.B. Frühstück, Bettwäsche) und den Wechselkursen.

Die Preise sind im internationalen Jugendherbergshandbuch zu ersehen. Für jede Jugendherberge, in der Sie reservieren möchten, berechnen wir für einen Aufenthalt bis zu sechs Tagen und für maximal neun Personen eine Servicegebühr von zehn DM. (Bei der Buchung mehrerer Personen bitte auch das Alter der Begleitpersonen angeben. In den meisten Jugendherbergen können keine Doppel- oder Familienzimmer gebucht werden.)

Folgende Jugendherbergen sind diesem Netz angeschlossen:

Australien: . . . . .Adelaide, Brisbane, Melbourne, Sydney (2);
Belgien: . . . . .Antwerpen, Brügge, Brüssel, Gent;
Brasilien: . . . . .Rio de Janeiro;
Costa Rica: . . . . .San José;
Canada: . . . . .Banff, Calgary, Edmonton, Halifax, Jasper, Montreal, Ottawa, Quebec, Toronto, Vancouver;
England & Wales: . . . . . .Ambleside, Bath, Bristol, Cambridge, Canterbury, Cardiff, Dover, London (7), Oxford, Stratford-upon-Avon, Windsor, York;
Finnland: . . . . .Helsinki;
Dänemark: . . . . .Kopenhagen;
Deutschland: . . . . .Düsseldorf, München;
Frankreich: . . . .Aix-en-Provence, Arras, Boulogne-sur-Mer, Carcassonne, Chamonix, Grenoble, Lyon, Marseille, Montpellier, Paris (2), Poitiers, Rennes, Straßburg (2);
Hongkong: . . . . .Hongkong;
Indonesien: . . . . .Bali;
Nordirland: . . . .Ballygally, Belfast, Omagh, Castle Archdale, Londonderry, Cushendall, New Castle, Whitepark Bay;
Republik Irland: . . . . .Dublin;
Italien: . . . . .Florenz, Genua, Rom, Venedig, Salerno, Sorrento, Turin, Venedig;
Japan: . . . . .Kyoto (3), Nara, Tokio;
Luxemburg: . . . . .Luxemburg Stadt;
Niederlande: . . . . .Amsterdam (2), Rotterdam;
Neuseeland: . . . . .Auckland (2), Christchurch, Wellington;
Österreich: . . . . .Salzburg, Wien-Brigittenau;
Portugal: . . . . .Lissabon;
Schottland: . . . . .Edinburgh (2), Glasgow, Stirling, Inverness;
Schweden: . . . . .Göteborg, Stockholm;
Schweiz: . . . . . .Basel, Bönigen, Lausanne, Luzern, Montreux, Pontresina, Sion, St. Moritz, Zermatt, Zug, Zürich;
Spanien: . . . . .Barcelona;
USA: . . . . . .Boston, Los Angeles, Martha's Vineyard Island, Miami Beach, New York, San Francisco (2), Sausalito, Seattle, Washington.

✂ *(Bitte vollständig ausfüllen.)*

Bitte senden an: DJH, 32754 Detmold

Geburtsdatum ☐☐☐☐☐☐ männl. ☐ weibl. ☐

Vorname, Familienname

Straße und Hausnummer

Postleitzahl   Wohnort

Telefon Nr.   Mitglieds.-Nr.

Einzugsermächtigung
Um den Verwaltungsaufwand gering zu halten, wird dieser Service nur unter der Voraussetzung durchgeführt, daß Sie uns die Möglichkeit eröffnen, die Angaben des Rechnungsbetrages von ihrem Bankgiro- bzw. Postgirokonto vorzubuchen.

Die bestellten Leistungen sollen von meinem Konto abgebucht werden.

Bankleitzahl   Kontonummer   Geldinstitut

Datum / Unterschrift

☞ ☐ **IBN - Reservierung in der Jugendherberge**

JH ☐☐☐☐☐☐☐☐☐☐☐☐☐☐☐☐

Personenzahl (höchstens 9) ☐ davon männl. ☐ weibl. ☐

Alter der Personen ☐☐ ☐☐ ☐☐ ☐☐ ☐☐ ☐☐ ☐☐

vom ☐☐☐ (Anreisetag) bis ☐☐☐ (Abreisetag)

"Globetrotter buchen über International Booking Network" from *Jugendherberge*. Reprinted by permission of *Deutsches Jugendherbergswerk Hauptverband*.

Copyright © by Holt, Rinehart and Winston. All rights reserved.

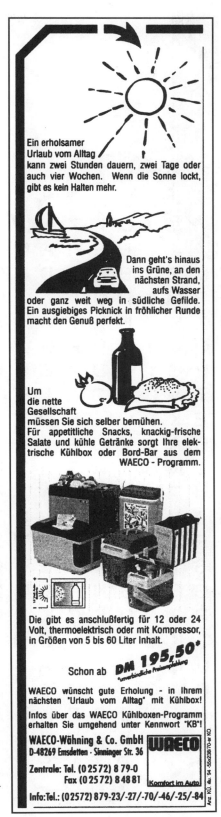

REALIA

Advertisement, "Ein erholsamer
Urlaub...WAECO" from *Focus*. Reprinted
by permission of ***Zett-Emm GmbH.***

Copyright © by Holt, Rinehart and Winston. All rights reserved.

Realia 2-3

Auf dieser Seite siehst Du die Bundesrepublik
Deutschland. Doch sind hier keine Städte,
Dörfer, Straßen oder Flüsse, sondern
Buchstaben. Wir haben Städtenamen in unse-
rer „Landkarte" versteckt. Du sollst sie suchen.
Aber Vorsicht: Du mußt waagerecht, senkrecht,
von unten nach oben, von hinten nach vorne
und umgekehrt lesen. Eine Hilfe: Die Namen
sind ungefähr dort, wo die Städte liegen. Und
diese Städte sollst Du suchen: Kiel, Rostock,
Hamburg, Bremen, Dresden, Schwerin, Berlin,
Potsdam, Hannover, Kassel, Dortmund, Koeln,
Bonn, Frankfurt, Saarbruecken, Nuernberg,
Passau, Stuttgart, Muenchen.

```
          G H
        S B K
        V C I Z       H M P
          U E H A M B U R G
      N E M E R B L F D S Q B O I P
      W E R M K H U I J C D E S P E
      B C X S E H K I T H A R T O
      P L O K J A D F G W U L O T L
      B U R G I N D A S E E I C S T
      D O R T M U N D L I R O N K D E P
      A U N B E K P O I E N I N I C A S S
      N U N T R A S V U S T N I G A M M E
      S O K O E L N S E W S N E D S E R D C
      P C S C H U T T R Z A W E R D N E
      S S O M A V I E L K M U T S
      E M A F R A N K F U R T S
      T C O N S T I B A B E L O
      U S S E G R E B N R E U N
      I S A A R B R U E C K E N L
        L O K O R I V E M A L
        Z U M B E I U A S S A P O
        T R A G T T U T S A A M
        S A G E N B O R K U N G
        S T I N N E H C N E U M
          H D T V F R
```

Wordpuzzle "Auf dieser Seite siehst Du die Bundesrepublik…" from *Juma: das Jugendmagazin*. Reprinted by permission of **Tiefdruck Schwann-Bagel GmbH.**

Copyright © by Holt, Rinehart and Winston. All rights reserved.

Realia 2-1: International Booking Network brochure

1. **Reading** Ask students to skim the information first for meaning, picking out familiar words and phrases. Tell them to look for keywords and context clues to give them the general meaning. Then have them read it through again and list the vocabulary they don't know on a separate sheet of paper. Have students check the vocabulary in a German/English dictionary. Go over the vocabulary with the class, and then read the ad again.

2. **Group Work/Writing** Several students are planning a summer trip together. They can visit as many places as they wish. Have each group decide on an itinerary. Then they will draw a map identifying their route. On the map, or on separate sheets of paper, they can draw (or paste pictures from magazines of) the sights they might see and the hostels where they might stay. Ask them to write a caption for each picture and a brief description of each leg of their travel route on the map. Give each group several copies of the reservation card and ask them to fill out one for each **Jugendherberge** in which they plan to stay.

3. **Thinking Critically** Ask students to compare and contrast the advantages and disadvantages of hotels versus youth hostels.

4. **Listening** Describe a destination and ask the students how many youth hostels are available in that country. You can make this more challenging by describing the country in detail rather than naming it.

5. **Reading/Role-playing** First ask students to read the material and to highlight or rewrite the important information and rules given, eg: membership information, written confirmation notice, pricing, etc. Then have pairs of students prepare skits which they then present to the class. One person in the pair will call the International Booking Network for information. The other will be the person responsible for giving out complete and accurate information.

Realia 2-2: WAECO cooler ad

1. **Reading (Visual/Tactile learners)** Make enough photocopies of the ad for each student in the class. Cut the ads so that the pictures and texts are separate. Place complete sets (i.e., pictures plus texts) in envelopes. Give each student his or her own complete (but separated) ad. Tell students to re-paste the ad, matching the texts with pictures and putting the elements into a logical sequence. When students have finished, display the original ad so that they can see how close their ads are to the original.

2. **Listening** Tell the class about a spontaneous trip you have taken or ask one or two students to tell about a spontaneous trip they, their family, or their friends have taken. Based on what is said about the time of year and the travel route, query the class about the kinds of clothes and foods that would have been appropriate for the trip. What activities would you have been likely to do on the trip? (For example, if it were a winter ski trip, the kinds of foods and clothing taken, as well as the activities, would have been quite different than if it were a summer beach trip.)

Copyright © by Holt, Rinehart and Winston. All rights reserved.

(For example, if it were a winter ski trip, the kinds of foods and clothing taken, as well as the activities, would have been quite different than if it were a summer beach trip.)

3. **Writing** Have each student imagine that he or she is taking a trip to a favorite (or fantasized) destination. Ask students to write an ad for the WAECO coolers for that destination, adding as many graphics and pertinent descriptions as desired. Encourage students to use elements that are different from those contained in the original ad.

4. **Writing (Slower pace)** First, on an overhead transparency, have the students underline key words in the original ad. You might wish to use a specific color for each type of word: red for verbs, blue for nouns, and green for adjectives. Adverbs should be underlined in orange. Connectors can be joined by a black arrow or bridge, etc. Then provide students with travel and geographic magazines, scissors, paper or posterboard, and paste, and have them create a vacation photo album. You may want to set a minimum or maximum for the number of the pictures used. Tell them to use at least one complete sentence as a caption to explain each picture. Remind them of the target vocabulary. You may tell them to set the action in the past, present, or future.

5. **Pair Work/Speaking** One member of the pair will be a salesperson for WAECO coolers. The setting may be at the WAECO market outlet. The other student in the pair is a customer describing his or her vacation plans. The salesperson and the customer must come to an agreement on the best size and voltage of the cooler. (Props are desirable for tactile and kinesthetic learners.) You may choose to have several pairs role-play for the whole class as a listening activity.

Realia 2-3: Word search

1. **Thinking Critically** Remove the text from the upper left hand corner. Tell students that they are searching for the names of German cities. Ask students if they can determine a context clue that makes it easier to find the names of the cities.

2. **Listening** After students have found the names of the cities, describe some major features of the cities (**liegt an der Nordsee; Hauptstadt von ...; usw.**) and then their locations on the map. Challenge students to guess the name of each city as early as possible in your description, based on the city's features rather than on its location.

3. **Writing (Tactile/Visual learners)** Have students design their own word search using target vocabulary. Tell them to stay with a single theme, such as foods. Then ask them to illustrate each of the hidden words somewhere on the page. They may choose whether or not to put the pictures near the words. Photocopy each word search created so that students may exchange word searches.

4. **Writing (Challenge)** Have students imagine that they are spending three weeks in Germany. They have a Eurail pass and can take the train to any city in Germany. Have them write a letter home describing what they have done and where they have been at the end of two weeks. Include in the letter their plans for the remaining week. The goal of their trip is to see as many German cities as they can during the three-week period, but their trip should be based on a logical and practical plan.

Copyright © by Holt, Rinehart and Winston. All rights reserved.

REALIA

Wellness '94

Die sanften Fitness-Methoden

Wellness heißt das neue Zauberwort und bedeutet ganzheitliches Wohlgefühl, die totale Harmonie zwischen Körper, Geist und Seele. Um sich rundum wohlzufühlen in seiner Haut ist es notwendig, Stress abzubauen, neue Energie zu tanken und der Seele die notwendigen Streicheleinheiten zu geben. Heute weiß man, daß sich „Wellness" am besten mit sanften Methoden erreichen läßt, statt mit schweißtreibendem Body-Building im Fitness-Studio. Der Mann von heute rückt etwaigen Problemzonen auf die sanfte Tour zu Leibe, zum Beispiel mit „Callanetics", einer neuartigen Methode zum Abspecken ohne forciertes Fastenprogramm. Hierbei wird auf Kosten der Fettzellen Muskelmasse aufgebaut. Auf sanfte Art fit werden, läßt sich bei-

spielsweise auch mit einer Farb-Therapie erreichen. Wer deren wohltuende Wirkung schon einmal am eigenen Leib zu spüren bekam, wird kaum daran zweifeln, daß Farben die Stimmung, die Gemütslage und das Verhalten des Menschen positiv beeinflussen. Mit gezielter Farbtherapie können selbst die Symptome von Migräne, Schlaflosigkeit und hohem Blutdruck deutlich gelindert werden. Auch die traditionelle chinesische Akupunktur zählt zu den sanften Wellness-Therapien, ebenso Sauna-Wickelkuren, Lymphdrainagen und Entspannungsmethoden wie Yoga und autogenes Training, die bereits in vielen Gesundheitszentren und Kurhotels angeboten werden. Fazit: Mann geht sanften Zeiten entgegen. Doch keine Sorge: Zum Softie wird Mann deshalb nicht. ■

Copyright © by Holt, Rinehart and Winston. All rights reserved.

Realia 3-2

MEIN CONTACTLINSEN-AUSTAUSCHSYSTEM
VON augenblick

Meine Vorteile bei augenblick

NUR DM 24,90 im Monat

- *jedes 1/2 Jahr neue Contactlinsen*
- *Nachkauf bei Verlust nur DM 30,50 pro Stück*
- *regelmäßige Nachkontrollen inklusive*
- *keine Chance für Ablagerungen*
- *immer meine aktuelle Linsenstärke*
- *immer optimale Sehschärfe für meine Augen*

Deshalb: augenblick - für meine Sicherheit

 augenblick

Michael Dauber Optik
Brillen • Lupen • Contactlinsen • vergrößernde Sehhilfen
Brücknerstraße 6 • 97080 Würzburg • Tel. 0931-2 67 07

Advertisement, "Mein Contactlinsen-Austauschsystem von augenblick," from *Zeltival: Schampus auf dem Campus!*. Reprinted by permission of **Augenblick Michael Dauber Optik.**

Copyright © by Holt, Rinehart and Winston. All rights reserved.

VOTUM DER WIRTSCHAFT

Wie bekomme ich den Job?

Was für den Erfolg eines Bewerbungsgesprächs ausschlaggebend ist, sehen Erstbewerber und personalverantwortliche Unternehmer offensichtlich sehr unterschiedlich.

Fast alle der 400 befragten Studenten in einem Abschlußsemester glauben an die Bedeutung der äußeren Erscheinung.

Für die Mehrzahl der rund 200 von FOCUS exklusiv befragten Unternehmer in Deutschland sind jedoch Persönlichkeit und Offenheit des Bewerbers wesentlich wichtiger.

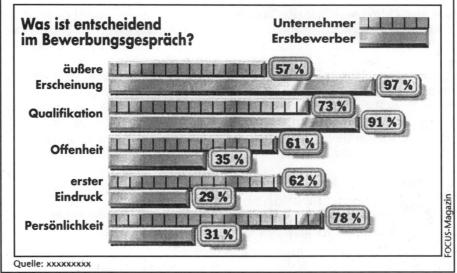

Was ist entscheidend im Bewerbungsgespräch?

Unternehmer
Erstbewerber

	Unternehmer	Erstbewerber
äußere Erscheinung	57 %	97 %
Qualifikation	73 %	91 %
Offenheit	61 %	35 %
erster Eindruck	62 %	29 %
Persönlichkeit	78 %	31 %

FOCUS-Magazin

Quelle: xxxxxxxxx

Graph "Wie bekomme ich den Job?" from *Focus*. Reprinted by permission of **Burda Syndication**.

REALIA

Copyright © by Holt, Rinehart and Winston. All rights reserved.

Realia 3-1: Wellness '94 article

1. **Reading** Show only the heading and sub-heading to students. Each student is to jot down a list of words he or she might expect to find in the text. From the individual lists, compile a complete class list on the chalkboard or on an overhead transparency. Then have the students read the text for content. They will highlight any words that match exactly or are essentially the same as the words on their list. (You may wish to turn this into a game and award points for each word they guessed correctly. Also, the point system can be based on the simplicity or complexity of the words. Some reward might be in order for a predetermined number of points, either awarded to the whole class or the individual with the most points.)

2. **Speaking** By asking questions, start an open class discussion in which students share any experiences they or their family and friends have had with soft exercise, color therapy, acupuncture, etc. Solicit students' opinions regarding the benefits of these experiences.

3. **Thinking Critically** Ask students to compare and contrast "hard" exercises and therapies to the newer "soft" wellness methods. What makes an exercise or therapy "hard" or "soft"? Have students analyze the strengths and weaknesses of each. Based on the strengths and weaknesses they listed, have students design a new program synthesizing the best features of each approach.

4. **Speaking/Thinking Critically/Writing** Drawing on the idea of color therapy, ask students to brainstorm some common expressions involving color as a metaphor, for example, "seeing red," "singing the blues," "a gray area," etc. Both the terms bright and dull, which refer to colors, also refer to a person's alertness. Ask students to draw inferences from these expressions and to write in past, present, or future tense about the way color has already affected them, is affecting them, or how they think it might affect them in the future. As an added challenge, ask them to look around at the colors of the walls, their own clothes, to think about the colors in their own rooms at home, and to say how these could be changed for the better or worse.

Realia 3-2: Ad for contact lenses

1. **Listening** Before showing the ad, read the content to the class. Ask them to tell you what the ad is about. Query for specifics.

2. **Writing/Speaking** Ask students to use the information they have just learned in the listening activity above to write an ad for contact lenses containing all the basic information. The ads will then be read aloud to the class. You may wish them to design the ad complete with illustration, logo, and attractive layout. (These ads will be used later in the **Thinking Critically** activity.)

Copyright © by Holt, Rinehart and Winston. All rights reserved.

3. **Reading** After students have had a chance to read their ads to the class, show the realia. Have them check content and spelling against the original ad.

4. **Thinking Critically/Speaking** Have students compare the layout, logo, and design of the actual ad to the ones they created. Ask them if some are more effective than others. If they find some more effective, ask them to say why. You may wish to have them then re-design their ads based on the insights gleaned from this discussion.

Realia 3-3: The article „Wie bekomme ich den Job?"

1. **Reading** Without showing students the graph, have them read the article. Tell them to underline key words that, by themselves, would indicate what the article is about. Make a complete class list of those words on the chalkboard.

2. **Speaking** Students have read that openness and personality are more important to interviewers than appearance. Tell them the five attributes that were surveyed and ask each student to put these in order of importance. This will lead to a class discussion about why one quality is considered more important than another. If the class does not come to a consensus, they may vote on the ranking. Then show them the actual results of the survey and rank the attributes from one to five. If the results differ from the class consensus, more discussion may follow.

3. **Speaking (Role-playing)** Assign several students to be job interviewers and the rest of the students to be students applying for a position, a description of which you have decided upon in advance. If possible, have available a few articles appropriate to a business setting to use as props (for example, telephone, clipboard, interview forms). You may also want to have the "job candidates" dress appropriately for the interview. After the interviewers have talked to their candidates, have them tell the class which person gets the job and why. Then have the candidates talk about why they think they did or did not get the job.

4. **Writing** Based on the above activity, each person will write about the interviewing experience both from the subjective viewpoint of the interviewee, and the objective viewpoint of the interviewer evaluating the performance of the other person. Have them use the criteria given in the article in descending order of importance for both evaluations.

R E A L I A

Copyright © by Holt, Rinehart and Winston. All rights reserved.

Realia 4-1

Wo gehöre ich hin?

1970 ist mein Vater als Gastarbeiter nach Deutschland gekommen. Er wollte etwas Geld verdienen und so schnell wie möglich nach Hause. Aus diesem „so schnell wie möglich" sind 22 Jahre geworden. Er hat seine schönste Zeit des Lebens damit verbracht, für die deutsche Industrie zu arbeiten und tut es immer noch. Ich bin seit 16 Jahren in Deutschland und besuche zur Zeit ein Gymnasium. Bis jetzt war ich sehr zufrieden, aber plötzlich werde ich mit dem Problem des Ausländerhasses konfrontiert. Man spricht mich auf offener Straße an und sagt, daß die Ausländer den Deutschen die Arbeit, die Wohnungen und sogar die Frauen wegnehmen. Die steigende Gewalt der rechtsradikalen Jugendlichen beunruhigt mich. Ich möchte so schnell wie möglich zurück in meine Heimat, die Türkei. Aber dort beschimpft man mich als „Deutschländer". „Geh doch in dein Deutschland", heißt es. Wo soll ich jetzt hin? Wo ist denn nun der Ort, wo ich hingehöre?

Emine. P. aus der Türkei, 16 Jahre, Kassel

Was soll das Theater?

Ich hatte noch nie richtige Probleme mit Deutschen. Trotzdem bin ich für viele Deutsche „nur eine Ausländerin". Letztens war ich in einem Supermarkt. Ein Deutscher hat sich vorgedrängelt und dann auch noch so getan, als sei er im Recht. Als Ausländerin habe ich oft erkennen können, daß es gute und weniger gute Deutsche gibt. Warum geben sich viele nicht ein bißchen mehr Mühe und versuchen, uns besser kennenzulernen? Was haben die meisten Ausländer den Deutschen wirklich getan? Sie helfen bei der „Dreckarbeit". Ich hoffe, daß wir Ausländer auf Dauer nicht als zweitklassig angesehen werden, denn es gibt keine zweitklassigen Menschen. In 178 Ländern sind die Deutschen selbst Ausländer. Tut nicht so, als wärt Ihr alleine auf der Welt. Was, also, soll das ganze Theater?

Giovana L. aus Italien, Frankfurt

"Wo gehöre ich hin?" and "Was soll das Theater?" from *JUMA: das Jugendmagazin.* Reprinted by permission of **Tiefdruck Schwann-Bagel GmbH.**

Copyright © by Holt, Rinehart and Winston. All rights reserved.

STREIT AM ZAUN

■ Rund eine halbe Million Prozesse pro Jahr, so eine Schätzung des Deutschen Mieterbundes, werden zwischen Nachbarn geführt. Oft ist der Anlaß gering-

fügig oder sogar skurril: der angeblich zu große Schatten eines Birnbaums, ein schimpfender Papagei, ein aus der Gartenmauer ragender Nagel ...

Zwei Gärten, zwei Nachbarn. Wenn sich der eine Garten-besitzer über den anderen ärgert, hat das folgende Gründe:

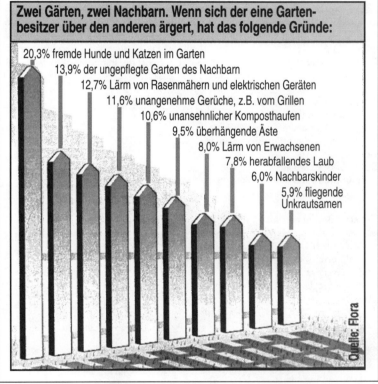

20,3% fremde Hunde und Katzen im Garten
13,9% der ungepflegte Garten des Nachbarn
12,7% Lärm von Rasenmähern und elektrischen Geräten
11,6% unangenehme Gerüche, z.B. vom Grillen
10,6% unansehnlicher Komposthaufen
9,5% überhängende Äste
8,0% Lärm von Erwachsenen
7,8% herabfallendes Laub
6,0% Nachbarskinder
5,9% fliegende Unkrautsamen

Quelle: Flora

"Streit am Zaun" from *Brigitta*. Reprinted by permission of ***Gruner & Jahr, Hamburg.***

Copyright © by Holt, Rinehart and Winston. All rights reserved.

REALIA

Realia 4-3

Wie benimmst du dich?

1 Auf einer Party benimmt sich jemand sehr unhöflich zu Dir.
a) Du bist verletzt und zeigst das auch. Du erzählst es den anderen.
b) Du bist genauso unhöflich.
c) Du ärgerst Dich nicht. Du drehst Dich um und sprichst mit netteren Leuten.

2 Jemand versucht, Dich zu belügen.
a) Du reagierst nicht. Du erzählst anderen, daß die Person lügt.
b) Du sprichst ihn direkt an und fragst ihn, warum er lügt.
c) Du fragst vorsichtig, was wirklich passiert ist.

3 Einer aus Deiner Klasse will Dir etwas erzählen. Ein Freund hat ihn gebeten, es nicht weiter zu erzählen.
a) Du hörst zu, denn Du bist neugierig geworden.
b) Du erzählst es weiter.
c) Es ist für Dich ein Bruch des Vertrauens. Darum willst Du es nicht hören.

4 Dein Bruder erzählt Dir etwas über sein Lieblingsthema. Es langweilt Dich fürchterlich.
a) Du unterbrichst ihn und versuchst, das Thema zu wechseln.
b) Du sagst nur: „Das hast Du schon einmal erzählt."
c) Du hörst zu. So lernt er auch das Zuhören.

5 Jemand hat eine feste Meinung. Du kannst beweisen, daß er sich irrt. Trotzdem bleibt er bei seiner Meinung.
a) Du bleibst ganz cool. Du sagst aber weiter, daß er unrecht hat.
b) Du protestierst laut und nennst ihn „einen Dummkopf".
c) Du sagst nichts. Du denkst: „Er wird schon merken, daß er unrecht hat."

6 Du triffst jemanden, der gerade eine große Enttäuschung erlebt hat.
a) Du meinst: „Das hätte ich dir gleich sagen können", und so behandelst Du ihn auch.
b) Du bittest ihn, alles zu erzählen. Du glaubst, das hilft ihm.
c) Du behandelst ihn normal. Du versuchst, ihn von seinem Problem abzulenken.

7 Du besuchst einen Freund im Krankenhaus. Er hat eine sehr ernste Krankheit.
a) Du paßt Dich der Krankenhaus-Atmosphäre an: Du sprichst leise und bedauerst ihn.
b) Du versuchst, ihn zu ermuntern: „Es wird schon wieder besser!"
c) Du benimmst Dich ganz normal. Du sprichst mit ihm über alles, was ihn interessiert.

Punkte

1. a – 5,	b – 7,	c – 10
2. a – 3,	b – 10,	c – 8
3. a – 5,	b – 3,	c – 10
4. a – 5,	b – 7,	c – 10
5. a – 10,	b – 3,	c – 8
6. a – 3,	b – 10,	c – 8
7. a – 3,	b – 8,	c – 10

TESTERGEBNIS

70 – 60 Punkte: Du kannst Dich sehr gut benehmen. Man spricht gerne mit Dir, denn Du fällst fast nie aus der Rolle. Manchmal aber versteckst Du Dich hinter gesellschaftlichen Sitten.

59 – 49 Punkte: Meistens sagst Du das Richtige. Du bist höflich, die anderen mögen Dich. Versuche, bei Deinen Freunden nicht nur höflich zu sein.

48 – 38 Punkte: Du hast kein schlechtes Benehmen, doch manchmal schätzt Du die Situation falsch ein. Du bist unsicher, ob Du das Richtige sagst. Du rettest Dich aus peinlichen Situationen mit Offenheit und guter Laune.

37 – 25 Punkte: Gesellschaftliche Sitten sind nichts für Dich. Manchmal läßt Du Dir das Wort nicht verbieten. Eigentlich ist das eine gute Eigenschaft. Versuche aber, mehr Rücksicht auf die Gefühle anderer Leute zu nehmen.

Test "Auf einer Party…" from *JUMA: das Jugendmagazin.* Reprinted by permission of **Tiefdruck Schwann-Bagel GmbH.**

Copyright © by Holt, Rinehart and Winston. All rights reserved.

Realia 4-1: The letters „Wo gehöre ich hin?" and „Was soll das Theater?"

1. **Speaking** Before reading the letters, ask students to recall a situation in which they might have been the "unfamiliar" element, either as a foreigner in another land or the newcomer in a neighborhood or classroom. Ask them to talk about how it felt and if they were eventually assimilated. Can they imagine what it would be like always to feel like an outsider?

2. **Listening/Speaking** Read the article **Wo gehöre ich hin?** to the class. Ask the students to answer questions about the age, nationality, educational level, and attitude of the boy who wrote the article, and about his father's occupation, age when he arrived in Germany, etc.

3. **Reading (Slower pace)** Have students read the article **Was soll das Theater?** through once, just to find familiar words. Ask each student to write down any words he or she does not know. Then have them read the article again for content, picking out key words that reveal the general meaning. In a third reading, ask the students to guess the meaning, based on context, of the words they did not know. Follow this with either dictionary work to check their guesses or go over the lists together as a class.

4. **Reading/Thinking Critically** Ask students to compare and contrast the similarities and differences between the two letters. Can they think of other situations where they have witnessed a 'them and us' mentality? Have students think about what might be some of the causes for people treating other people as 'second class citizens'. Have them think about and then discuss some of the possible solutions to this situation.

5. **Writing** Tell the students to write their own letters to the editor, expressing either a personal experience of being an outsider or responding to one of the two actual letters. They may respond sympathetically or unsympathetically.

6. **Group Work (Role-playing)** Give each group enough time to prepare a short skit. Each skit is to deal with a situation in which one person is a foreigner or an outsider. Suggest that they present as many points of view as possible; for instance, the outsider, a sympathetic friend, a counselor or advisor, activist(s) for or against equal rights, a legislator, an educator, etc.

Realia 4-2: The article „Streit am Zaun"

1. **Reading** Ask students to read the short article and to determine the tense in which it is written, and to differentiate between text that is essential to the meaning of the article and that which is non-essential.

Copyright © by Holt, Rinehart and Winston. All rights reserved.

2. **Listening/Speaking** Suggest that there are probably areas of disagreement among students that have to do with boundary issues. Have them brainstorm as many such areas of discord as they can. (For example, dropping belongings onto someone else's desk, crowding your neighbors at the lockers, bumping into people in the hallways during class change, etc.) Ask them to discuss the sorts of incidents that bother them and what they can do about these situations.

3. **Writing (Group Work)** Have students create a questionnaire from their list of grievances. Ask them to conduct a survey among students and teachers. Then have them create their own bar graph indicating the percentage of people upset by each situation. Encourage them to come up with a creative graphic, like the picket fence, appropriate to a school setting (e.g. a line of lockers, or rulers, pencils, etc.).

4. **Group Work (Role-playing)** Have students set up a mock courtroom and try individual cases. You may wish to write each grievance on a slip of paper and have each group pick one at random from a grab bag. Challenge them to come up with win/win solutions to the problems that create a harmonious rather than an acrimonious atmosphere among the participants.

Realia 4-3: The magazine test „Wie benimmst du dich?"

1. **Listening/Speaking (Challenge)** Do not show the test to the students but tell them the gist of it. Read the answer choices to the students and ask them to guess what the questions might be. Do this one number at a time. After everyone has had a chance to guess each question, read the actual question to them.

2. **Reading/Listening (Slower pace)** Give each student a copy of the test. Allow time for students to scan the test for general content. Go over new vocabulary and make sure that students understand the questions. Then allow students to pair up, taking turns reading the questions to each other. The person reading will keep score and inform the other of his or her points. Do not reveal the score results section until after this process is complete.

3. **Group Work (Role-playing)** Divide the class into small groups. Each group will act out one or more of the questions from the test. Each one should be done three times: each time students will perform a different one of the three responses given on the test.

4. **Writing** Ask students to write about a real situation similar to, but not exactly the same as, those situations given on the test. They can write about the event in a descriptive paragraph (or two), as a fictional story, a play, a poem, or a cartoon with text.

5. **Thinking Critically** Have students come up with three category names for the type of responses given, for example, aggressive, assertive, passive, angry, impatient, calm, etc. After they have come up with three basic categories, ask them to list each of the responses under the appropriate heading. After they have finished, give them the test results and have them discuss the results in small groups. Have students tell the class in which of the categories they fit.

Copyright © by Holt, Rinehart and Winston. All rights reserved.

Name _____ Klasse _____ Datum _____

3. Wehrdienst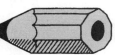

Worum geht es?	Was ist zu tun?
1. Wehrerfassung	der Aufforderung Folge leisten
2. Musterung	der Aufforderung Folge leisten, Atteste mitbringen
3. Zurückstellung vom Wehrdienst	mit Formular o. formlos beantragen
4. Freistellung vom Wehrdienst für Helfer im Katastrophenschutz	mit Formular beantragen
5. Unabkömmlichkeitsstellung	Antrag durch Arbeitgeber mit Formular
6. Unterhaltssicherung bei Grundwehrdienst, Wehrübungen und Zivildienst	mit Formular beantragen
7. Gesundheitsschäden durch den Wehrdienst	bei der Truppe nachfragen, ob bereits ein Verfahren auf Feststellung der Wehrdienstbeschädigung eingeleitet wurde; mit Formular Entschädigung beantragen
8. Kriegsdienstverweigerung	schriftlich beantragen unter Berufung auf Artikel 4 Absatz 3 Grundgesetz mit ausführlicher Begründung, Lebenslauf u. polizeilichem Führungszeugnis (nicht älter als drei Monate)

From table "Wehrdienst" from *Bayerischer Behördenwegweiser*. Reprinted by permission of **Bayerisches Staatsministerium des Innern, Odeonsplatz 3, 80539 München, Germany.**

Copyright © by Holt, Rinehart and Winston. All rights reserved.

Realia 5-2

 **Fahrschule Wagner**
Talstraße 275
56077 Koblenz
Tel: 0261-832157

Fahrschulausweis

für Herrn/Frau/Fräulein _____

_____ Kl. _____

Diesen Ausweis unbedingt zu den Unterrichts- und
Fahrstunden mitbringen.

_____

Meine nächsten Übungsfahrten:

Tag	Dat.	Uhrz.	Tag	Dat.	Uhrz.	Tag	Dat.	Uhrz.

Am theoretischen Unterricht teilgenommen:

Datum	Datum	Datum	Datum

Bezahlte Beträge

Datum	Betrag	Quittung

Copyright © by Holt, Rinehart and Winston. All rights reserved.

Name _____ Klasse _____ Datum _____

Ein Weg zur Entscheidung:
Schritt für Schritt

Welche Voraussetzungen bringe ich mit?
(Interessen, Werte, Fähigkeiten, Kenntnisse, Qualifikationen)
Ausgangssituation

Welchen Beruf möchte ich ergreifen?
Zielvorstellung

Kann ich mit meinen Voraussetzungen das angestrebte Berufsziel erreichen?
Vergleich Ausgangssituation mit Zielvorstellung

Welchen Ausbildungsweg muß ich gehen, um mein Berufsziel zu erreichen? Gibt es mehrere Wege?

Kann ich mit dem gewählten Ausbildungsweg auch andere Berufsziele erreichen?
Lösungsplanung

So mache ich es!
ENTSCHEIDUNG

Chart "Ein Weg zur Entscheidung", Bundesanstalt für Arbeit (Hrsg), from *abi Berufswahl-Magazin*. Sonderheft für Schülerinnen und Schüler der 9. und 10. an Gymnasien und Gesamtschulen. Reprinted by permission of **Transmedia Projekt & Verlagsgesellschaft mbH, Mannheim 1994.**

Copyright © by Holt, Rinehart and Winston. All rights reserved.

Realia 5-1: Wehrdienst instructions

1. **Reading** Explain to students that the government often uses a bureaucratic vocabulary which may not be familiar to them. Ask them to read copies of the instruction sheet and to highlight unfamiliar words. Then either help them with meanings or have them use dictionaries to obtain correct definitions.

2. **Writing** Students will have noted that in most cases some sort of form(s) (**Formular**) are necessary for each of the instructions. Ask them to design a form or forms that would obtain the kind of information they imagine would be required of them in these different situations. You may want to have them work in small groups, with each group choosing one of the situations for which to create form(s). Make copies of each form and ask students to fill them out as if they were applying for consideration in one or more of the situations listed.

3. **Speaking** This is a good opportunity to allow the students to express their opinions, hopes, and concerns about military service and its alternatives in an open discussion, or perhaps staged as a debate.

Realia 5-2: Fahrschulausweis

1. **Listening** Compare the relatively inexpensive driver's education programs of the U.S.A. to the costly private driving lessons available in Germany. Explain in German the use of the record card at the **Fahrschule Wagner** and, based on the information you give them, ask the students to fill out a copy of the card as if they were students there.

2. **Speaking (Role-playing)** Using a toy phone as a prop, ask students to role-play calling the **Fahrschule Wagner** for information regarding scheduling of theory classes, driving practice times, and cost. (You may wish to have them do this before filling out the cards.)

3. **Writing (Thinking Critically)** Ask students to write about the possible advantages and disadvantages of attending a driving school, as opposed to having an older sibling or a parent teach them.

Realia: 5-3: „Ein Weg zur Entscheidung" graphic

1. **Reading** Go over the flow chart with students to be sure that they understand all content. Make a complete list on the chalkboard of any vocabulary the class does not know and give definitions or have the class use a dictionary to look up unfamiliar words.

2. **Speaking (Thinking Critically)** Call on students to tell you the differences between the categories listed in the first box.

Copyright © by Holt, Rinehart and Winston. All rights reserved.

3. **Writing** Once students are clear about the differences between the categories, ask them to head a sheet of paper with five columns (in German): interests, values, knowledge, abilities, and qualifications. Each student is to list as many attributes in each column as possible. Encourage students to list even those interests, such as playing computer games and listening to music, that are not usually associated with a career. Tell them that many great careers were started by innovators who found a new way to use what they already loved to do. (For example, Kentucky Fried Chicken was started by Col. Sanders after retirement. He was unhappy with the amount of his social security check. He loved making chicken and everyone he knew loved his recipe. He knocked on over 1,000 doors before someone liked his idea well enough to sell his chicken and split the profits). After listing everything they can think of, have them underline all those that apply to the profession they have been considering. After that, ask them to brainstorm any profession, no matter how unlikely, that might include even more items than those that were already underlined. Then encourage them to complete all the steps, on separate sheets of paper, for each of the possible professions rather than just the one or two they had previously considered.

4. **Pair Work** Allow students time to share with each other the discoveries they made while doing the above activity, and to ask for and give advice. Ask them to say whether they feel their options are greater, and if they feel confident that they can make a good choice from among those options.

REALIA

Copyright © by Holt, Rinehart and Winston. All rights reserved.

Realia 6-1

SPIELEN UND DISKUTIEREN:
Über Videospiele kommen die Schüler ins Gespräch
SPIELANALYSE

Ergebnisse der Schülerbefragung

„Wenn es mir nicht gut geht, kann mich das Spiel wieder aufbauen."

	Trifft zu	Sowohl als auch	Trifft nicht zu
Jungen	35%	20%	45%
Mädchen	23%	7%	70%

„Ich würde mein Freizeitverhalten ändern, um das Spiel zu beherrschen."

Jungen	8%	24%	68%
Mädchen	15%		85%

„Ich bin sicher, daß das Spiel meine Leistungsfähigkeit verbessern kann."

Jungen	95%	1%	4%
Mädchen	59%	7%	34%

„Die ‚Helden' des Spiels können ein Vorbild sein."

Jungen	29%	20%	51%
Mädchen	6%	15%	79%

„Das Spiel kann mir helfen, Freundschaften zu schließen."

Jungen	71%	9%	20%
Mädchen	51%	16%	33%

„Durch das Spiel werde ich geschickter."

Jungen	76%	11%	13%
Mädchen	85%	6%	9%

„Durch das Spiel fühle ich mich als Versager."

Jungen	7%	2%	91%
Mädchen	11%	5%	84%

Quelle: Günter Blasini

Graph "Spielanalyse" from *Focus*.
Reprinted by permission of **Burda Syndication**.

Copyright © by Holt, Rinehart and Winston. All rights reserved.

Name _____ Klasse _____ Datum _____

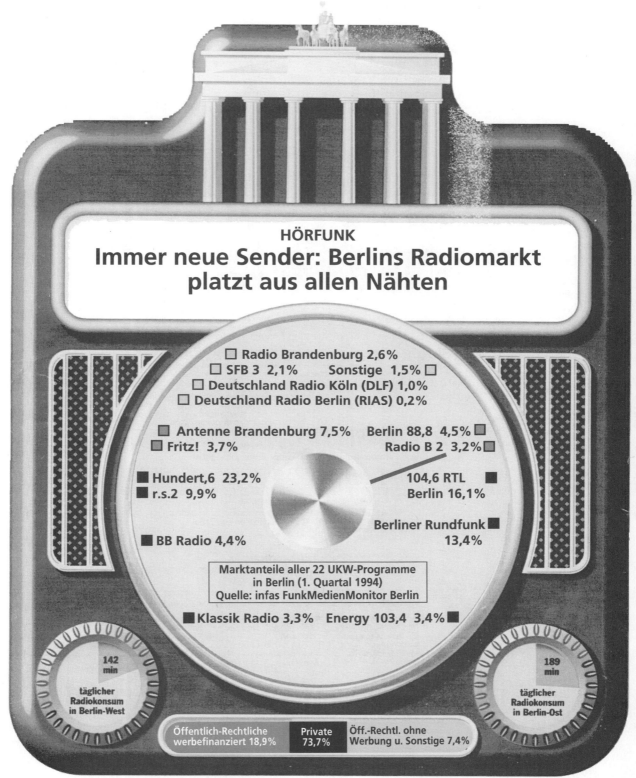

HÖRFUNK
Immer neue Sender: Berlins Radiomarkt platzt aus allen Nähten

☐ Radio Brandenburg 2,6%
☐ SFB 3 2,1%   Sonstige 1,5% ☐
☐ Deutschland Radio Köln (DLF) 1,0%
☐ Deutschland Radio Berlin (RIAS) 0,2%

■ Antenne Brandenburg 7,5%   Berlin 88,8 4,5% ■
■ Fritz! 3,7%   Radio B 2 3,2% ■

■ Hundert,6 23,2%   104,6 RTL ■
■ r.s.2 9,9%   Berlin 16,1%

■ BB Radio 4,4%   Berliner Rundfunk ■
                                13,4%

Marktanteile aller 22 UKW-Programme
in Berlin (1. Quartal 1994)
Quelle: infas FunkMedienMonitor Berlin

■ Klassik Radio 3,3% Energy 103,4 3,4% ■

142 min
täglicher Radiokonsum in Berlin-West

189 min
täglicher Radiokonsum in Berlin-Ost

Öffentlich-Rechtliche werbefinanziert 18,9% Private 73,7% Öff.-Rechtl. ohne Werbung u. Sonstige 7,4%

REALIA

Graph "Hörfunk. Immer neue Sender: Berlins Radiomarkt platzt aus allen Nähten." from *Focus.* Reprinted by permission of ***Burda Syndication.***

Copyright © by Holt, Rinehart and Winston. All rights reserved.

Realia 6-3

Wer warnt die Bürger?

Um die Warnung der Bevölkerung zu gewährleisten, hat der Bund im Rahmen des Zivilschutzes einen eigenen Warndienst aufgebaut.

Regelmäßig zweimal im Jahr macht er auf sich aufmerksam. Im März und im September werden die Sirenen auf ihre Funktionstüchtigkeit geprüft.

Sie haben sie sicher schon gehört. Wisse Sie auch, was sie bedeuten?

Rundfunkgerät einschalten
– auf Durchsagen achten.

1 Minute Heulton

Sie werden über Art und Ausmaß eines Unglücksfalles, einer Katastrophe oder eines sonstigen wichtigen Ereignisses informiert und bekommen gezielte Verhaltenshinweise.

Feueralarm
Signal nur zur Alarmierung der Feuerwehr.

1 Minute Dauerton – zweimal unterbrochen

Für den hoffentlich nie eintretenden Verteidigungsfall – der aber trotz aller Friedensbemühungen leider nicht ganz ausgeschlossen werden kann – sind folgende Signale vorgesehen:

Luftalarm
Warnung vor Luftangriffen.

1 Minute Heulton

ABC-Alarm
Warnung vor radioaktiven, biologischen oder chemischen Gefahren.

1 Minute Heulton – zweimal unterbrochen, nach 30 Sekunden Pause – Wiederholung

Entwarnung
Beendigung der Gefahr nach Luft- bzw. ABC-Alarm.

1 Minute Dauerton

Verhalten bei Sirenenalarm (außer bei Signal „Feueralarm")

● Achten Sie auf Rundfunkdurchsagen.
● Befolgen Sie die Anordnungen der Behörden.

● Informieren Sie auch Ihre Nachbarn über die Durchsagen und Anordnungen.
● Helfen Sie Ihren Nachbarn.

● Telefonieren Sie nur, falls nötig; fassen Sie sich kurz.
● Sind Sie selbst und Ihre Nachbarn von Schäden nicht betroffen:

Bleiben Sie dem Schadensgebiet fern.
● Suchen Sie bei Luft- oder ABC-Alarm einen Schutzraum oder den Keller auf.

Graph "Sirenensignale" from brochure *Sicherer leben*. Reprinted by permission of **Bundesministerium des Innern.**

Copyright © by Holt, Rinehart and Winston. All rights reserved.

Realia 6-1: The Spielanalyse

1. **Reading** Present the bar charts to students, allowing them to see that the charts compare boys' and girls' answers to various questions. Don't let students see the questions. Ask the students to guess what the subject of the survey might be. Write all their suggestions on the chalkboard or on a transparency. When they have listed as many ideas as they can, reveal the questions to them. Ask them to identify the words and phrases used repeatedly for the purpose of ascertaining information for the survey. Ask them if there is any indication of the age, background, or number of students queried.

2. **Writing (Group Work)** Have students design a questionnaire that includes the questions shown in the **Spielanalyse,** and to answer the questions themselves as honestly as possible. They might also query another group of students to get more objective statistics. Have them do a group project creating a large display graph indicating class results. How do their statistics compare to the original? (The results could be applied to the following speaking activity.)

3. **Speaking (Thinking Critically)** Ask students what results they anticipated, and if the results they received differed from those they expected. Can they conclude from this survey whether gender or culture is the more powerful influence? If they think they can, can they say why one is more powerful than the other? Also, ask the students if they would have asked different questions from those on the survey. Did the people conducting the survey understand their topic well enough to ask the most relevant questions? Does it matter how many people were asked and what their ages and backgrounds were?

4. **Speaking** Use one or more of the questions as the basis for a class discussion.

5. **Writing** Have each student choose a topic that is timely and pertinent to teens and to create a survey on that topic. Each survey should have at least seven questions that are relevant to the topic.

6. **Writing (Challenge)** Have each student apply his or her own survey outside the classroom and return at a later date with both a chart showing the results and a "newspaper article," describing how, why, when, where, and with whom the survey was conducted and giving the highlights of its results.

7. **Listening** Have students read their articles to the class. Encourage them to draw their charts on transparencies or on posterboard to serve as visual aids.

Realia 6-2: The Berlins Radiomarkt information

1. **Reading/Listening (Thinking Critically)** Show the realia to students. Have them look at it while you read the information on it to them. Afterwards they can analyze, either verbally or in writing, the information it presents (e.g.: location, types of radio stations, the comparison of east/west listening habits, the overall purpose of the information, etc.). Ask them what related information it doesn't supply (type of station—whether rock or classical, etc.; demographics of people who listen, peak listening times, etc.).

Copyright © by Holt, Rinehart and Winston. All rights reserved.

2. **Speaking** Ask students if radio plays an important role in their lives. What percentage of their overall time is devoted to reading, watching, or listening to the different types of media? What percentage of this time is spent listening to the radio? Discussions can lead in many directions (for example: the quality of programs, the language of popular music, the importance of lyrics and the feelings they invoke, the advantages and disadvantages of radio compared to TV or other media, etc.).

3. **Speaking (Role-playing)** Divide the class into pairs. Assign each pair a type of radio show to do (or have them pick one out of a grab bag). Possibilities include news, sports, weather, talk show, music, etc. (You may have to have more than one pair do the same type of show.) After you have given them time to write a short radio show, have pairs come up one at a time and transmit "live from Radiostation _____." If possible, bring in a microphone to use as a prop.

4. **Listening** Ask students questions based on the radio reports and shows given by their classmates. If necessary to increase proficiency and to use target vocabulary, create your own report or program (or use an actual recorded German radio program).

5. **Writing** Students may rephrase the information contained in the realia to create a short article about radio in Germany.

Realia 6-3: Sirenen-Signale information

1. **Writing** Prior to showing the realia, ask each student to think about and list five different emergency situations. When they have completed this activity, draw three columns on the chalkboard or on a transparency. The columns should be headed (in German): Personal, Local, General. Call on students to tell (or come up and write) the emergencies they listed and in which category each emergency belongs. Continue until a class list has been formulated.

2. **Speaking** Ask students to discuss what they should do in these emergencies. If they don't know, for which type(s) of emergency are they least prepared?

3. **Reading** Have students read the information individually for general meaning, highlighting or listing the unfamiliar words. Go over the meaning of new vocabulary with the whole class and have students read the realia again. Tell them to study the types of signals and what purpose they serve. After they have done this, have them put the information away. Then you should announce each type of emergency and call on a student to make the appropriate signal sounds.

4. **Reading/Speaking (Thinking Critically)** If students had to tell someone quickly what to do in case of an actual emergency, but didn't have time to describe the different types of signals and what they represent, what most important information could they give? Ask them to go over the information once more to find the most important advice. Ask them to synthesize the salient information into a few brief sentences and to share it with the class or a partner.

Copyright © by Holt, Rinehart and Winston. All rights reserved.

REALIA

KUDDELMUDDEL MÄRCHEN SPIEL

1 — Es war einmal ...
- ein kleines Mädchen. Das ...
- ein schöner Prinz. Der ...
- ein grünes Männchen. Das ...
- ein alter Esel. Der ...
- eine böse Königin. Die ...
- (eine Person ausdenken). Der/die/das ...

2
- hatte immer zuwenig Geld.
- hatte immer Hunger.
- hatte eine lange Nase.
- war viel zu dick.
- hatte ziemlich viele Probleme.
- hatte null Bock auf gar nichts.

3 — Eines Tages ...
- wollte er/sie/es die totale action.
- suchte er/sie/es wieder einmal seinen linken Schuh.
- bekam er/sie/es Besuch von der Schwiegermutter.
- war wieder einmal der Kühlschrank leer.
- hatte er/sie/es wieder einmal die große Wut.
- fiel sein/ihr Walkman in einen tiefen Brunnen.

4 — Da ging er/sie/es ...
- in den tiefen Wald,...
- in die Schule,...
- über die sieben Berge,...
- in die Disco,...
- in die weite Welt hinaus,...
- in den Zoo,...

5
- um einen Freund (eine Freundin) zu finden.
- um Hilfe zu holen.
- um auch mal ins Fernsehen zu kommen.
- um das Fürchten zu lernen.
- um das große Glück zu finden.
- um sein/ihr Unglück zu vergessen.

6 — Plötzlich begegnete ihm/ihr ...
- ein Deutschlehrer. Der fragte:
- ein großer Wolf. Der brummte:
- ein dicker Frosch. Der quakte:
- ein Zauberer. Der murmelte:
- eine alte Hexe. Die zischte:
- eine schöne Fee. Die flüsterte:

7
- „Knusper, knusper, knäuschen, wer knuspert an meinem Häuschen?"
- „Warum hast du so ein schrecklich großes Maul?"
- „Was rumpelt und pumpelt in meinem Bauch?"
- „Entschuldigen Sie bitte, wo geht's denn hier zum Bahnhof?"
- „Hey, kannst du mir mal fünf Mark leihen?"
- „Können Sie mir bitte sagen, wie spät es ist?"

8 — Der/die/das ... (Person) antwortete:
- „Komm lieber mit nach Bremen, da wollen wir Stadtmusikanten werden."
- „Zeigen Sie erst mal ihren Dienstausweis!"
- „Ich darf nicht mit fremden Leuten reden."
- „Verzeihung, ich spreche kein Deutsch."
- „Tut mir leid, ich bin fremd hier."
- „Können Sie mich nicht was Leichteres fragen?"

9
- Da holte der/die ... (Figur) einen roten Apfel aus der Tasche und sagte:
- Da zog der/die ... (Figur) einen goldenen Schuh vom Fuß und sprach:
- Da zog der/die ... (Figur) einen Hasen aus dem Hut und meinte:
- Da zog der/die ... (Figur) Kuchen und Wein aus der Manteltasche und rief:
- Da schüttete der/die ... (Figur) eine Schüssel Linsen auf den Boden und sagte:
- Da hatte der/die ... (Figur) plötzlich einen Hamburger in der Hand und rief:

10 — ...und du wirst schon sehen."
- „Bring' das zur nächsten Polizeistation,..."
- „Gib das deiner Großmutter,..."
- „Gib das in deiner Schule ab,..."
- „Leg das unter dein Kopfkissen,..."
- „Nimm dies und trage es immer bei dir,..."
- „Geh' und schenke das dem ersten Menschen, den du siehst,..."

11 — Das tat der/die/das ... (Person), und am nächsten Tag ...
- stand Tarzan vor der Tür.
- lag vor dem Haus ein Berg von Bratwürsten.
- lag vor seinem/ihrem Bett ein Sack voll Gummibärchen.
- hatte er/sie grüne Haare.
- stand ein Kamel vor seinem/ihrem Bett.
- kam die ganze Geschichte im Fernsehen.

12 — Da freute sich der/die/das ... (Person), denn ...
- nun hatte alle Not ein Ende.
- jetzt konnte er/sie/es endlich heiraten.
- nun war sein/ihr größter Wunsch erfüllt.
- jetzt konnte er/sie/es endlich seine/ihre Reise nach Deutschland machen.
- von diesem Tag an hatte er/sie/es viele Freunde.
- Humor ist, wenn man trotzdem lacht!

From game, "Kuddelmuddel," from *Jugendscala Sonderheft Alles Märchen?* Copyright © by Frankfurter Societäts-Druckerei. Reprinted by permission of **Deutschland Redaktion**.

Komm mit! Level 3, Chapter 7   Activities for Communication **81**

Copyright © by Holt, Rinehart and Winston. All rights reserved.

Realia 7-2

Advertisement "Der Poliboy-Schwung" from *Bunte*. Reprinted by permission of **Poliboy, Brandt & Walther D-28831 Bremen**.

Copyright © by Holt, Rinehart and Winston. All rights reserved.

Advertisement "Almdudler," from *Bravo*. Reprinted by permission of **Almdudler Deutschland, Marketing & Communication GmbH, Lehmkuhlstraße 21, D-32108 Bad Salzuflen**.

Copyright © by Holt, Rinehart and Winston. All rights reserved.

Realia 7-1: The Kuddelmuddel game

1. **Reading** Show the realia, but do not go over the content with students. Cover the numbers. Ask students to read individually for the main ideas. Tell them that the paragraphs are in incorrect sequence and that they are to arrange the paragraphs in the correct order. If they need a clue, tell them that the paragraphs are related to the sequence of events common to many fairy tales. As they read the paragraphs for main ideas, encourage them to guess words they don't know based on context. Ask them to keep a record of those words and what they think they mean. Afterwards, show the numbers and have them check their proposed sequence against the correct one. Also, go over the meaning of the words they guessed.

1. **Speaking** Have students sit in a large circle. Choose a student to begin the story with **Es war einmal ...** and to choose the main character. Pass the story from one student to the next, following the sequence given on the realia. (This sequence could be written on the chalkboard or transparency so that students may have a large visual aid.) Each person's addition should logically proceed from the previous contribution. Tell them they may use the suggestions given on the realia; however, encourage them to use their own variation or a completely new idea. Suggest that they keep the story going as long as possible, as long as it still makes sense.

2. **Writing/Reading (Slower Pace)** Have each student write on an index card an idea for each section. Tell them to use at least one complete sentence for each of the 12 sections on one side and to number the card on the other side, following the sequence given on the realia. Collect the cards and put them into 12 numbered grab bags. Have the first student pick a card from number 1 and read it aloud, the next from number 2, and so on, until a complete random story has been completed.

3. **Writing (Challenge)** Ask students to choose any familiar fairy tale character (e.g.: Cinderella, The Little Tailor, Pinocchio, Hansel or Gretel, etc.), and to say how they or someone they know well resembles that character and what similar but real-life challenges they may have faced.

4. **Thinking Critically** This may be a written or spoken activity, or might even be done for visual/tactile learners as a flow chart with illustrations. Ask students to choose a favorite book, movie, or TV program and to create a main plot sequence, dividing it up into as many "sections" as necessary. Remind them that this should be designed so that anyone could take the 'lead in' and be able to create a plot to fit that book, movie, or TV show.

5. **Listening** Read a fairy tale to students and ask them to indicate by a show of hands whenever the next section of the plot sequence, as given in the realia, has begun. Be sure to choose a fairy tale that closely matches the sequence given in the realia. To make this even more challenging, you might read the fairy tale out of sequence and ask the students to indicate which section of the plot you have just given before going on to the next one.

REALIA

Komm mit! Level 3, Chapter 7

Copyright © by Holt, Rinehart and Winston. All rights reserved.

Realia 7-2: The Poliboy ad

1. **Reading** Have students read the advertisement. Ask them to list the main points that the Poliboy people are trying to get across to the public. Remind them not to ignore the graphics, as this is a very important part of the message.

2. **Writing (Visual/Tactile learners)** Have students design their own ads, either re-designing the Poliboy ad or creating one for another familiar product.

3. **Challenge (Auditory learners)** Ask students to create a catchy advertising jingle for Poliboy. Perhaps the more outgoing students would be willing to perform their jingles.

4. **Thinking Critically/Writing** Have students display their ads after they have completed them. The class can then rate them for effectiveness on a scale of 1 to 10. To do so, students must analyze what it is that makes an ad effective (e.g.: visual appeal, information, logo, catchy phrase, etc.). Once they have categorized those areas that are important to a successful ad, ask them to synthesize this new information to create a better ad.

5. **Reading/Speaking** Ask students to tell you what information is given on the pictures of the bottles that is not given in the written text.

Realia 7-3: The Almdudler ad

1. **Writing** Cover the words in the word bubble. Ask each student to write what he or she thinks would be appropriate, given the rest of the ad. You might wish them to create words for the female figure as well. Compile a list of different responses on a transparency or on the chalkboard. Have students choose five or so that they think are most fitting.

2. **Reading** Uncover the word bubble. Students should recognize that this is a German (Bavarian) dialect. There is enough similarity between the dialect and the German they know in order for them to guess what the word bubble in the ad says.

3. **Thinking Critically/Speaking** Have students compare and contrast this ad for Almdudler and the previous ad for Poliboy. Have them go beyond the obvious comparisons (one is larger than the other) and speak about style, emphasis, lettering, logo, impact, etc.

4. **Role-playing (Pair Work)** Have pairs of students create a skit based on the idea that the characters in the ad have come to life in that setting. Tell them that the skit must include the product. Allow time for students to act out their skit for the class. (An old mineral water bottle—label removed, a glass, a straw, some plastic flowers, and an item or two reminiscent of **Tracht** would be very helpful to this activity, especially for kinesthetic/tactile learners.)

Copyright © by Holt, Rinehart and Winston. All rights reserved.

Realia 8-1

AMERIKANER IM SCHWARZWALD

Menzenschwand. Im Rahmen des German American Partnership Program verbrachten 17- bis 19jährige Schüler aus Minnesota eine Woche im Schwarzwald. Sie waren in der Jugendherberge Menzenschwand unterge- bracht und von der dorti- gen Gastfreundschaft ebenso angetan wie vom Ambiente und dem Pro- gramm, das sie unter an- derem in den Dom zu St. Blasien, verschiedene Museen und auf Wande- rungen führte.

Europäische Jugendwochen

Heidelberg. Die europäi- schen Jugendwochen, die der DJH-Landesverband Baden seit zehn Jahren veranstaltet, fanden in diesem Jahr in der Ju- gendherberge Heidelberg statt. 36 junge Leute aus ganz Europa nahmen zwei Wochen lang an Vorträgen, Arbeitsgrup- pen und Diskussionen zu verschiedenen Themen teil. Inhalte: das Europa- parlament, West-Ost-Ge- fälle in der Wirtschaft, Ausländerfeindlichkeit. Daneben gab es themen- bezogene Ausflüge, und es blieb auch Zeit für Kultur- und Freizeitakti- vitäten.

DJH-Landesverband Baden e.V.
Weinweg 43
76137 Karlsruhe
Tel. 07 21/96 21 00
Fax: 61 34 70

"Amerikaner im Schwarzwald" from *Jugendherberge*. Reprinted by permission of *Deutsches Jugendherbergswerk Hauptverband*.

Copyright © by Holt, Rinehart and Winston. All rights reserved.

Kuckucksuhren – typisch deutsch?

Sie gelten als „typisch deutsch" und haben nicht nur in Deutschland einen Riesenerfolg: 1990/91 wurden ca. 500.000 Kuckucksuhren hergestellt. Zwei Drittel davon waren für den Export bestimmt.

Was die einen bewundern, ist für andere Kitsch; manche kaufen sie sogar nur aus diesem Grund – und das bei Preisen von 80 bis 2000 Mark.

Seit Mitte des vorigen Jahrhunderts sind Bahnwärterhäuschen Vorbild für die Gehäuseform. Als Ornamente dienen Vögel, Blätter, Äste, Hirsche oder Adler aus geschnitztem Holz. Unter dem Gehäuse hängen Gewichte in Form von Tannenzapfen.

Das erste Modell baute 1750 Franz Anton Ketterer in der Nähe von Triberg im Schwarzwald. Dort finden sich noch heute die meisten der 12 Herstellerfirmen. Sie haben über 100 handgeschnitzte Modelle im Angebot.

Das Besondere einer Kuckucksuhr: Zu jeder halben und vollen Stunde öffnet sich im Holzgehäuse ein Türchen, und ein Holzvogel imitiert durch Pfeifen einen Kuckucksruf so oft, wie die Stunde geschlagen hat.

COUPON
Bitte ausschneiden und auf Postkarte kleben! Absender nicht vergessen!

DAS IST FÜR MICH TYPISCH DEUTSCH:

_____
_____
_____

An die
Redaktion JUMA/TIP
Stichwort: typisch deutsch
Frankfurter Str. 128
D-W 5000 Köln 80

"Kuckucksuhren-typisch deutsch?" from TIP, 2/93, April 1993, p. 37. Reprinted by permission of *Tiefdruck Schwann-Bagel GmbH*.

Copyright © by Holt, Rinehart and Winston. All rights reserved.

Realia 8-3

UNI - (K)EINE FRAUENSACHE !?
DISKUSSIONSRUNDE DER JUSO HOCHSCHULGRUPPE ZUR GLEICHSTELLUNG AN DER UNI

„Diskriminierung von Frauen? Doch nicht an der Uni!", leider ist dies noch immer eine verbreitete Meinung. Dabei sprechen die Zahlen für sich. Uni Würzburg: 45.5% Studentinnen – 3.5% Professorinnen.

Unser Anliegen ist es, eine solche Diskrepanz zu erklären, allgemein auf die Frauenproblematik an der Uni aufmerksam zu machen und Lösungsvorschläge zu diskutieren. Dazu haben wir kompetente Gesprächspartnerinnen eingeladen.

Im Rahmen einer Gerprächsrunde wird u.a., informiert und diskutiert über die Arbeit einer Frauenbeauftragten, über Hintergründe und gesamtgesellschaftliche Zusammenhänge der Frauenproblematik an der Uni, über Lösungsvorschläge und Perspektiven und alles, was Euch zu diesem Thema interessiert.

DIENSTAG, 14. JUNI, 17:30 UHR

AFRIKA - DER VERGESSENE KONTINENT
VERANSTALTUNG DES INFO-MARKTS EINE-WELT

Trotz Trommelworkshops und Afrodisco bleiben unsere Vorstellungen von Afrika sehr vage. Der von Armut, Naturkatastrophen und Kriegen gebeutelte Krisenkontinent, findet auch in Politik und Wirtschaft trotz historischer Verantwortung aus der Kolonialzeit, z.B. Ruanda, kaum Beachtung. Die Veranstaltung will anhand von einigen afrikanischen Produzentinnengruppen aus dem Bereich des alternativen Handels einzelne Problemfelder und Lösungsansätze vorstellen. Referenten: Martin Lang (Bildungsreferent) und Michael Röhm (ehemaliger Entwicklungshelfer).

DONNERSTAG, 16. JUNI, 14:00 UHR

YEU Yeu D.G. e.V., Youth for Exchange and Unity ist eine kleine, aber feine Gruppe von Leuten, deren Hauptanliegen internationale Begegnungen und interkulturelles Lernen sind. Yeu veranstaltet Jugendtreffen mit TeilnehmerInnen aus der ganzen Welt. Themen dabei sind unter anderem: Rassismus, Medien, Erwachsenwerden in verschiedenen Kulturen, Jugend-Macht-Geld. Die Gruppe hat in ihrem 10jährigen Bestehen bereits zahlreiche Auslandskontakte aufgebaut. Außerdem hält YEU jeden ersten Samstag im Monat das internationale Frühstück im Café Cairo ab und bringt sich so auch auf der lokalen Ebene in die Jugendarbeit ein.

FREITAG, 10. JUNI, 15:00 UHR

"UNI- (K)EINE FRAUENSACHE!?," "AFRIKA - DER VERGESSENE KONTINENT," and "YEU" from *Zeltival - Programmheft*. Reprinted by permission of *Studierenden Vertretung Universitaet, Würzburg*.

Copyright © by Holt, Rinehart and Winston. All rights reserved.

Realia 8-1: The article „Amerikaner im Schwarzwald"

1. **Thinking Critically** Based solely on the main headline, ask students to infer the content of the article. Then show them the main subhead. Can they derive more about the article from that? Have students predict vocabulary that they are likely to find in the article.

2. **Reading** Once the students have completed the **Thinking Critically** activity above, allow them to read the article. Ask them to underline, highlight, or list any vocabulary that they do not understand. Is there new vocabulary that they are able to understand because of its context? As a whole class activity, have students figure out the words they don't know. As much as possible, allow the students to help each other glean the meanings of the new vocabulary.

3. **Writing** Ask students to devise their own tests to check comprehension of the material. These may be multiple choice, fill in the blank, true or false, or other methods of their choice. Though the tests are written, you may want to give them the option of giving each other the tests orally.

4. **Pair Work** Have pairs of students administer their tests to each other.

5. **Speaking (Group Work)** Have students imagine that they are attending the European Youth Week with other young people from all parts of Europe. Assign to each group or have students choose a discussion theme from the article. Move about the room so that you can help students express ideas and opinions regarding their topics.

6. **Group Work** Allow groups of students to prepare a large-scale scrapbook page (on large paper or posterboard) with drawings, pasted pictures, and mock memorabilia from their imagined trip. These items might include train tickets, hotel brochures, ticket stubs, pictures of people they met, postcards showing historical and other famous landmarks, etc.

Realia 8-2: The Kuckucksuhren ad

1. **Listening** Before showing the realia to students, read just the portion that describes what the cuckoo clock does, but don't name it. Ask students to guess what you are describing. You might also want them to suggest a paragraph heading for what you have just read. If they need help, ask them to think about a question that the information could be answering.

2. **Reading/Writing** Tell students that this article is full of facts and that an outline is an excellent way to organize facts during or after reading. Outlines help separate the essential from the non-essential and prioritize information. Ask students to formulate an outline based on the material presented in this realia.

3. **Speaking (Thinking Critically-Discussion)** What is the headline asking? Is the cuckoo clock typically German? What else can students think of that is typically German? Students may notice qualities common to things that are typically German. If they were to analyze those qualities (for example, craftsmanship, materials, ingredients, design, etc.), could they then synthesize them into a single statement about typically German items? This can be done as a whole class activity or in small to medium-size groups.

Copyright © by Holt, Rinehart and Winston. All rights reserved.

4. **Speaking (Challenge)** If you have students with intermediate or advanced speaking skills, ask them to describe a cuckoo clock. They should include as much detail as possible. Some students might want to describe what the clock looks like, while others might want to tell the class how a cuckoo clock works.

Realia 8-3: The Seminare/Vorträge flyer

1. **Thinking Critically** Ask students to look only at the headings to each paragraph, one at a time. Based on the headings, ask students to predict what content is likely to be included in the text that follows. Write their predictions on the board or on an overhead transparency.

2. **Reading** First, have students scan the text to see if they can find any of the key words, or phrases from the **Thinking Critically** activity. Then go over any vocabulary that is unfamiliar. Afterwards, have the students read the text thoroughly and answer questions prepared beforehand. Questions for the first section might include: What, if any, sarcasm is present in the first section? What single statistic gives credence to the entire topic? What backgrounds will the speakers have? In the second section, questions might include: What aspects of African culture are known in Germany, according to the text? What does the writer mean by „vergessene"—is it meant literally here? What is a close approximation of the term „vergessene"? Does at least one of the speakers have "hands-on" experience with Africa? How do we know this? Ask students to look for vocabulary in the text that points to what the writer is implying. Who intends to address the problem?

3. **Writing** After reading the YEU section, tell each student or group of students to assume the role of an active member of YEU responsible for planning and promoting an activity that has international and intercultural implications. Students will borrow from the vocabulary, ideas, and format of the realia to advertise a significant topic of their choice. Encourage them to use a headline with or without a subhead that captures the content of the text. They are to give the event a time, date, and meeting place.

4. **Speaking/Pair Work** Have students imagine that this flyer is announcing events in their school. Have them take turns inviting their partners to attend one or more of the sessions. Their invitation should include information on what the session is about and when it takes place.

5. **Speaking/Listening (Role-playing)** You may wish to choose one or more of the best topics that the students have suggested in the **Writing** activity. If possible, set up the classroom to look like a café. Ask the students to treat the discussion, or, if a seminar, the presentation, as seriously as if it were an actual YEU event initiated by young people for young people. If done as a seminar, plan for a question-and-answer period, so that all students have a chance to participate. In any case, one person should serve as moderator to keep the discussion on track.

Copyright © by Holt, Rinehart and Winston. All rights reserved.

Danke! Mit dieser Marke helfen Sie, den tropischen Regenwald zu retten.

Dänemark, Österreich, Holland, 16,8 Millionen Hektar. Diese Fläche wird alljährlich im tropischen Regenwald zerstört. Schluß mit dem Raubbau fordert deshalb die aktuelle Sondermarke der Deutschen Bundespost. Der Zuschlag von 0,50 DM pro Mark trägt direkt zur Rettung des tropischen Regenwaldes bei.

So helfen Briefmarkensammler jetzt auch der Natur. Denn bereits seit 1919 unterstützen Sie mit den Wohlfahrtsbriefmarken z. B. die Katastrophen-, Kinder- oder Altenhilfe. Und mit den Ausgaben „Für den Sport" erleichtern Sie den deutschen Sportlern den Weg zur Spitze.

Wollen auch Sie sich für den Naturschutz einsetzen? Und gleichzeitig eine grenzenlose Themen-Vielfalt entdecken? Dann informieren Sie sich über das praktische Start-Abo vom Sammler-Service: Damit bekommen Sie alle neuen Briefmarken direkt ins Haus - 1992 für 79,25 DM, also im Schnitt für weniger als 7, - DM pro Monat. Schicken Sie uns einfach den ausgefüllten Teilnahmeschein - und Sie können viel gewinnen.

Wir verlosen
20 Framework City Bikes
- Handmade in Germany

Teilnahmeschein

Bitte ausgefüllt auf eine Postkarte kleben und bis zum 2. 7. 1992 einsenden an den Sammler-Service, Abt. Info-Versand, 4830 Gütersloh 100.

Wofür setzt sich die aktuelle Ausgabe der Deutschen Bundespost ein?
Für ☐ die Wohlfahrt ☐ den Sport
☐ den tropischen Regenwald

☐ Ich möchte nur am Gewinnspiel teilnehmen
Ich möchte weitere Informationen über
☐ das Briefmarkensammeln, denn ich bin noch kein Briefmarkensammler.
A 2601
☐ die Angebotsvielfalt des Sammler-Service, denn ich bin bereits Briefmarkensammler.
A 2609

Name

_____ 19
Vorname   Geburtsjahr

Straße

PLZ/Ort

Alle richtigen Einsendungen nehmen an der Verlosung teil. Der Rechtsweg ist ausgeschlossen. Teilnahmekarten gibt's auch in Ihrem Postamt.

RETTET DEN TROPISCHEN REGENWALD

DEUTSCHE BUNDESPOST

100 +50

Advertisement, "Danke! Mit dieser Marke helfen Sie, den tropischen Regenwald zu retten." from *stern magazin*. Reprinted by permission of ***Deutsche Bundespost Postdienst***.

REALIA

Copyright © by Holt, Rinehart and Winston. All rights reserved.

Realia 9-2

„Mensch, Dein Party-Müll steht mir bis zum Hals!"

Sicher kennen Sie das: nach der Party kommt der "Müllkater". Das muß nicht sein. Der Tip der Saison: Partys ohne Wegwerfteller und -bestecke. Sondern mit Porzellan, Gläsern und "richtigem" Besteck. Denken Sie daran. Gleich beim Einkauf für Ihre nächste Party.

Beim Müllvermeiden hilft Ihnen die neue Verpackungsverordnung des Bundesumweltministers. Denn sie verpflichtet Handel und Industrie, sämtliche Verpackungen zurückzunehmen oder wiederzuverwerten. Seit 1. April 1992 können Sie auch sogenannte Umverpackungen, wie z.B. die Kartons der Whiskey- und Cognacflaschen, also zusätzliche Kartonagen um bereits verpackte Waren, bei Ihrem Kaufmann an der Kasse zurücklassen. Und seit 1993 können Sie sogar alle Verpackungen zurückgeben, d.h. auch Chipstüten oder Erdnußdosen. Jetzt liegt's an Ihnen. Bevor uns der Müll über den Kopf wächst: Machen Sie Müll-Diät! Der Bundesumweltminister schickt Ihnen gerne weitere Informationen.

MACH MIT BEI DER MÜLL-DIÄT!

EINE INITIATIVE DES BUNDESUMWELTMINISTERS

Advertisement "Mensch, Dein Party-Müll steht mir bis zum Hals!" from *Brigitte*, vol. 2, October 1991. Reprinted by permission of the *Bundesumweltminister*.

Copyright © by Holt, Rinehart and Winston. All rights reserved.

Auch die kleinen
Sünden zählen

 Bevorzugen Sie beim Kauf Produkte, die bei der Herstellung, beim Gebrauch und bei der Beseitigung das Wasser möglichst wenig belasten. Achten Sie beim Einkauf auf den blauen „Umweltengel".

 Verwenden Sie Putz- und Reinigungsmittel sparsam. Viel kostet viel und schadet viel!

 Nutzen Sie die Kapazität Ihrer Waschmaschine und Ihres Geschirrspülers voll aus. So gelangen weniger Wasch- und Reinigungsmittel in die Gewässer.

 Nehmen Sie nur soviel Waschmittel, wie für den Härtebereich Ihres Wassers notwendig ist. Auskunft erteilt Ihr Wasserwerk.

 Alte Medikamente, Farben, Lacke, Lösungsmittel, Batterien, Kosmetika, Foto- und Hobbychemikalien gehören zur Sondermüll-Sammelstelle. Fragen Sie Ihre Gemeinde.

 Feste Abfälle – soweit sie nicht ohnehin der Wiederverwertung zugeführt werden – gehören in den Mülleimer; geeignete Küchenabfälle möglichst auf den Komposthaufen, keinesfalls ins Abwasser. Sie können nur mit großem Aufwand wieder aus dem Abwasser geholt werden.

Geben Sie Altöl bei der nächsten Tankstelle oder öffentlichen Sammelstelle ab. Es kostet Sie nur den Weg dorthin.

Waschen Sie Ihr Auto nie an einem Gewässer! Reinigungsmittel und Ölreste sind für das Leben am und im Wasser gefährlich.

"Auch die kleinen Sünden zählen" from the brochure *Das Wasser - Umweltschutz in Bayern*, p. 20. Reprinted by permission of **Bayerisches Staatsministerium für Landesentwicklung und Umweltfragen, Rosenkavalierplatz 2, 81925 München, Germany.**

REALIA

Copyright © by Holt, Rinehart and Winston. All rights reserved.

Using Realia 9-1, 9-2, 9-3

Realia 9-1: The Postdienst ad

1. **Listening/Speaking** First, ask your students (rhetorically) what a stamp, a bicycle, and rainforests have in common. Then read the realia to the class. Ask them the question again to check comprehension. Then ask them to talk about their ideas regarding protecting the rainforests. Ask them what other causes have been supported, how much money has been raised, how much the stamps cost, etc., according to the article. Would any of them be interested in participating in such a program?

2. **Group Work** Have small groups choose a political, environmental, or cultural cause similar to the one featured here. Each group is to design a stamp and write an article, along with deciding on what lottery prize to offer, to raise money for its cause.

3. **Challenge** Ask students to research and provide factual information substantiating the need for support, such as the fact that 16.8 million hectares of rainforest are lost each year.

Realia 9-2: The Party-Müll public service ad

1. **Reading/Thinking Critically** Have students read the realia completely through once. Ask them, in the context given, how the word „Mensch" is used. Is the headline meant to be taken literally? What similar expressions do we use in English and what mood do we seek to achieve when we use them? Why might the author use these words colloquially or as slang for this particular topic? What mood does the author want to achieve? (Answer: 'cool'/'with it') What is unusual about the request in this realia? (Answer: targeting "party trash" specifically) Have students read the article again and underline or highlight the recycling requirement that the German government has for commerce and industry. Compare and contrast this requirement to current American rules concerning packaging material.

2. **Writing** Have each student create a list of items he or she regularly uses at parties, either parties given or parties attended. The list could be divided into two columns: one for disposable items and one for non-disposables. If you wish, students might further categorize the items as plastic, paper, aluminum, etc. Ask them afterwards to write a few sentences indicating some changes in party habits that would better protect the environment.

3. **Speaking (Group Work)** Each student will bring his or her list of suggestions created in Activity 2. Each group will have time to select two or three of the best ideas, and a designated speaker will present those ideas to the whole class.

REALIA

Copyright © by Holt, Rinehart and Winston. All rights reserved.

Realia 9-3: The Umweltschutz in Bayern flyer

1. **Reading**   Have students underline or highlight words using a color or symbol code to indicate different parts of speech: red for verbs, blue for nouns, green for adjectives, orange for adverbs, and any color arrow or bridge beneath the word for prepositions and connectors, respectively. By looking at the verbs together and perhaps reading them aloud to students, lead them to discover that the majority of the sentences are commands. Are there any other kinds of sentences in the eight items? Ask students to indicate these. (For example, there are several declarative sentences.)

2. **Writing**   Now point out that the headline emphasizes negative behavior. A common English expression, 'every little bit counts,' has a more positive connotation. Ask the students to rewrite the headline and the eight items emphasizing a more positive, informative tone.

3. **Listening (Visual/Kinesthetic learners)**   Bring items mentioned in the realia (old medicine bottles, cosmetics, paint cans, detergent boxes, etc.) to class. Paste or draw a little blue angel on one or two of the items. Label containers to match the vocabulary in the realia (e.g. compost). Place signs in the classroom to stand for trash collection or recycling sites, as given in the realia. Call on one student at a time to mime each behavior, using the props, as you give one or other of the commands in random order. (You may have to modify the commands slightly so that students will be able to model the behavior. For example, for Number 2 you might say **Gebrauchen Sie wenig Putzmittel, wenn Sie das Bad säubern.**)

REALIA

Copyright © by Holt, Rinehart and Winston. All rights reserved.

Realia 10-1

KOMÖDIE
IM
BAYERISCHEN HOF

Abo-Telefon 0 89/29 16 05 30 und 29 16 16 33

BESTELLSCHEIN
KOMÖDIE IM BAYERISCHEN HOF
SPIELZEIT 1994/95

Hiermit bestelle(n) ich/wir

____ *Abend*-Abonnement(s) der Platzgruppe _____ ☐ Parkett

    Theatertag: ☐ Sonntag   ☐ Balkon

            ☐ Montag

            ☐ Dienstag

            ☐ Mittwoch

            ☐ Donnerstag

____ Wahl-Abonnement(s) der Platzgruppe _____ ☐ Parkett

____ Theatertage: Sonntag bis Donnerstag _____ ☐ Balkon

____ *Premieren*-Abonnement(s) der Platzgruppe _____ ☐ Parkett

                                                   ☐ Balkon

Das Abonnement verlängert sich automatisch, sofern keine
Kündigung bis zum 30.5. vorliegt.

Name, Vorname: _____

Straße, Ort: _____

_____

Telefon: _____

Beruf: _____

Unterschrift: _____

Bezahlung: ☐ Scheck   ☐ Überweisung   ☐ Bar

SPIELZEIT 1994/95

CABARET
Musical von Kander • Masteroff • Ebb
mit **GEORG PREUSSE, ANNETTE MAYER** u.a.
Orchester und Ballett
Inszenierung: Michael Wedekind
Bühne: Thomas Pekny

DAS KONZERT
Lustspiel von Hermann Bahr
mit **CHRISTIANE HÖRBIGER,
WOLFGANG HÜBSCH** u.a.
Inszenierung: Gerhard Tötschinger
Ausstattung: Thomas Pekny

DER REGENMACHER
Romantische Komödie von N. Richard Nash
mit **GERHART LIPPERT, HARTMUT RECK,
SASKIA VESTER** u.a.
Inszenierung: Karl Absenger
Ausstattung: Thomas Pekny

CANDIDA
Komödie von Bernard Shaw
mit **HEIDELINDE WEIS, FRANK HOFFMANN,
PASCAL BREUER** u.a.
Ausstattung: Thomas Pekny

LORBEEREN FÜR HERRN SCHÜTZ
Komödie von Jean Noel Fenwick
mit **BARBARA WUSSOW, ALBERT FORTELL** u.a.
Inszenierung: Klaus Wagner
Ausstattung: Thomas Pekny

LORIOTS DRAMATISCHE WERKE
TEIL II
von Vicco von Bülow
mit **GUNNAR MÖLLER,
CHRISTIANE HAMMACHER** u.a.
Inszenierung: Stefan Zimmermann
Ausstattung: Thomas Pekny

Flyer *Komödie im Bayerischen Hof.* Reprinted by permission of ***Komödie im Bayerischen Hof Theaterbetriebe Margit Bönisch GmbH,
Promenadeplatz 6, 80333 München.***

Copyright © by Holt, Rinehart and Winston. All rights reserved.

Nachtmusik
mit
stimmungsvoller
Illumination

im Hofgarten
   der Residenz Würzburg
Samstag,
   4. Juni, 21 Uhr
Samstag,
   25. Juni, 21 Uhr

im Schloßgarten Werneck
   Freitag,
   17. Juni, 20.30 Uhr

Promenadenplätze zu 10,- DM an den Abendkassen.
Bei ungünstiger Witterung findet das Konzert nur für Sitzplatzkarten-Inhaber
im Treppenhaus der Residenz bzw. in der kath. Pfarrkirche Werneck statt.
Auskünfte: Mozartfest-Büro · Haus zum Falken · Telefon (0931) 3 73 36

Advertisement, "Tanzender Schäfer," Signet des Mozartfestes Würzburg from *Umsonst & Draussen*. Reprinted by permission of **Kulturamt**.

Copyright © by Holt, Rinehart and Winston. All rights reserved.

Realia 10-3

Advertisement "Legende des Rock" from *WOM® Journal*. Reprinted by permission of *eastwest records GmbH Germany*.

Copyright © by Holt, Rinehart and Winston. All rights reserved.

Realia 10-1: The Komödie schedule

1. **Listening** Before showing the realia, pretend that you are doing a radio commercial for the 1994/95 season at **Komödie**. Include whatever supplementary background information you might know about the season's offerings as well as titles, authors and composers, and ticket information.

2. **Speaking** To check comprehension for the **Listening** portion, have the students role-play calling you (the theater agent) for show and ticket information based on what they heard you say. Instruct them to ask for background information. Afterwards, have students act out calling friends to invite them to one or more of the shows, and have them agree upon a show, date, and seating choice.

3. **Reading** Now have students take turns being the ticket agent and answer your questions, based on what they read from the schedule. When a few such conversations have been modeled, allow students to practice this in pairs.

4. **Writing** Students can practice taking information over the phone and filling out the form for the callers.

Realia 10-2: The Mozart Fest ad

1. **Listening** Before showing the realia to students, describe the rather unusual graphic to them. Ask them if they can guess what it might represent.

2. **Reading/Speaking** Show the realia to students and ask them to read the contents. After looking over the ad, ask them to explain how the graphic fits or doesn't fit.

3. **Writing** Play some of Mozart's music. Have students design their own ad for a live performance of that music accompanied by a light show. Tell each student to create a graphic or written description of the music to enhance the ad.

4. **Speaking (Group Work)** Have small groups of students plan a group outing to attend the show. Have them decide on a location and date, and agree on travel arrangements and activities before and after the show. Tell them they will need a back-up plan in the event of rain.

5. **Writing** Have students choose any of the three realia pieces in this chapter and write a letter to a friend or relative, telling him or her about a hypothetical performance attended.

6. **Reading** After the above **Listening** activity, have students scan the text for English words that have become part of the German lexicon.

Copyright © by Holt, Rinehart and Winston. All rights reserved.

Realia 10-3: The ad Legenden des Rock

1. **Critical Thinking**   Have students compare and contrast the different types of music in the three realia pieces for this chapter. Have them give as much information as possible regarding the complexity of the music, the time span the particular type of music covers, each type of music's likelihood of enduring in popularity, historical development, economic and cultural value, emotional and intellectual content, mode of delivery, mass appeal, technical aspects, etc. You might want to make a list of topics where comparisons can be made and let students choose the topic that most interests them.   Encourage them to think about the role of music in people's lives.

2. **Speaking**   Hold a debate or discussion regarding the relative merit of different kinds of music in contributing to culture and civilization.

3. **Speaking (Challenge)**   Ask individual students to tell about favorite pieces of music and the emotional or intellectual message they contain.

4. **Writing**   Have students choose any of the three realia pieces in this chapter and write a letter to a friend or relative, telling him or her about a hypothetical performance attended.

5. **Listening**   If possible, bring to class the lyrics of any of the songs listed from the Legends of Rock. Read the lyrics in English. Translate them into German and read those to students as well. Tell students to listen particularly for idiomatic expressions that do not translate well.

6. **Reading**   After the above **Listening** activity, have students scan the text for English words that have become part of the German vocabulary.

7. **Listening/Speaking**   Have students listen to various types of music (Mozart, Wagner, the Animals, etc.) and have them tell you in German how listening to that music makes them feel.

Copyright © by Holt, Rinehart and Winston. All rights reserved.

WER BEI UNS ANFÄNGT, MUSS SICH DURCH MEHR ALS 10.000 ARTIKEL DURCHBEISSEN.

Die leicht verdauliche Theorie: Jede Menge Artikel fürs Köpfchen.

Die schmackhafte Praxis: Bis zu 10.000 Artikel für Leib und Seele.

Keine Angst, es geht hier nicht um Unmengen von Gesetzbuch-Artikeln, die auswendig gelernt werden wollen. Es geht vielmehr um die vielen kleinen Dinge (genannt: Produkte oder Artikel), die man fürs tägliche Leben braucht.

Von A wie Apfelmus bis Z wie Zahncreme: Bis zu 10.000 dieser Artikel sind je nach Größe des Geschäfts für jedermann bei uns zu haben.

Und wer etwas mehr Interesse an ihnen hat und sich sogar vorstellen kann, daraus seinen Beruf zu machen, dem können wir einiges bieten. Zum Beispiel einen Ausbildungsplatz zum Kaufmann oder zur Kauffrau im Einzelhandel. Da lernt man erstmal 3 Jahre lang, wie man richtig ein- und verkauft.

Man lernt alles über die einzelnen Artikel. Man lernt beraten und verkaufen und ganz nebenbei jede Menge Menschen kennen. Und die Theorie, die nun einmal dazugehört, servieren wir so, daß sich keiner die Zähne daran ausbeißt.

Wenn Sie den nötigen Biß dafür haben, sollten Sie uns schreiben: **REWE-ZENTRAL AG, 5000 KÖLN 1, POSTFACH 10 15 28,** oder anrufen: **02 21/14 91 52.** Postwendend kommen dann alle Informationen zur Ausbildung als Kaufmann/-frau im Einzelhandel bei der REWE.

DIE REWE HANDELSGRUPPE: REWE · R-KAUF · HL-MARKT · GROKA · STÜSSGEN · GLOBUS · PETZ · BRÜCKEN · MINIMAL · KONTRA

Advertisement, "Wer bei uns anfängt, muss sich durch mehr als 10.000 Artikel durchbeißen." from *Popcorn.* Reprinted by permission of *REWE-Zentral AG, Köln.*

Copyright © by Holt, Rinehart and Winston. All rights reserved.

Was ist für dich bei einem Beruf wichtig?

- Ein Beruf, bei dem ich mich persönlich entfalten und kreativ sein kann
- Eine selbständige und verantwortungsvolle Tätigkeit
- Eine Arbeit, die immer wieder neue Aufgaben stellt
- Eine Arbeit, bei der ich meine Fähigkeiten einbringen kann
- Ein sicherer Arbeitsplatz

- Ein Beruf mit guten Verdienst- und Aufstiegsmöglichkeiten
- Eine Tätigkeit mit hohem Ansehen
- Ein Arbeitsplatz mit guten Arbeitsbedingungen
- Ein Beruf, bei dem ich auch viel Freizeit habe
- Eine Arbeit, bei der ich mit Menschen zu tun habe
- Ein Beruf, bei dem ich anderen helfen kann

"Was ist für dich bei einem Beruf wichtig?" Bundesanstalt für Arbeit (Hrsg), from *abi Berufswahl-Magazin*, Sonderheft für Schülerinnen und Schüler der 9. und 10. an Gymnasien und Gesamtschulen. Reprinted by permission of **Transmedia Projekt & Verlagsgesellschaft mbH, Mannheim 1994**.

Copyright © by Holt, Rinehart and Winston. All rights reserved.

Entdecken Sie Ihren Weg zum Erfolg

Sie wollen weiterkommen

und wissen, daß Sie eigentlich mehr aus sich machen können! Sie wollen

- Ihr Wissen erweitern ▪ selbstsicherer werden
- den beruflichen Anforderungen der Zukunft gewachsen sein
- privat und beruflich mehr erreichen.

Wir zeigen Ihnen, wie Sie Ihre Zukunfts-Chancen selbst verbessern. Neben Ihrem Beruf, ohne Verdienstausfall. Bequem von zu Hause aus, im Rahmen eines staatlich geprüften **Fernstudiums**.

Die FERNAKADEMIE für Erwachsenenbildung bietet rund 100 Fernstudiengänge mit unterschiedlichsten Berufs- und Bildungszielen an.

Nutzen Sie Ihre Chance – diese Vorteile überzeugen!

1. Sie studieren in Ruhe zu Hause, erhalten „Privatstunden per Brief".
2. Sie beginnen, wann Sie wollen und bestimmen Ihr Lerntempo selbst.
3. Sie sind in ständigem Kontakt mit Ihrem Studienleiter, der Ihre Fragen individuell beantwortet.
4. Sie studieren ohne Risiko – mit Widerrufs- und Kündigungsrecht.
5. Sie erhalten nach erfolgreichem Abschluß ein Zeugnis – wichtig auch für staatliche und öffentlich-rechtliche Prüfungen.

Fordern Sie unverbindlich unser neues, umfangreiches **GRATIS-STUDIENHANDBUCH 94/95** mit vielen für Sie wichtigen Informationen an: Per COUPON oder Telefon!

Wählen Sie Fernunterricht

SCHULABSCHLÜSSE

ABITUR	1001
Fachhochschulreife Technik	1101
Fachhochschulreife Wirtschaft	1201
Realschulabschluß	1301
Deutsch mit Literaturkunde	1410
AUTOR werden – schreiben lernen	1580

FREMDSPRACHEN

Englisch Grundkurs	2010
Englisch Vollehrgang	2020
Cambridge First Certificate in English	2131
Handelsenglisch	2220
Französisch	2420
Italienisch	2510
Russisch	2540
Spanisch	2520

COMPUTER/EDV

Grundlehrgang Datenverarbeitung	4010
Programmierer/in	4050
Programmiersprachen:	
– PASCAL	4150
– BASIC	4110
– COBOL, C	4180
Einführung und Programmierung in MS-DOS	4130
Textverarbeitung mit WORD	4140

WIRTSCHAFT

Staatl. gepr. Betriebswirt/in	3011
Bilanzbuchhalter/in	3210
Buchführung und Bilanz	3220
Geprüfte Sekretärin IHK	3510
Bürosachbearbeiter/in	3170
Fremdsprachenkorrespondent/in IHK in Englisch	2710
Verkaufsleiter/in	3340
Gepr. Anlage- und Vermögensberater/in	3530
Ausbildung der Ausbilder	3360
Management-Techniken/ Unternehmensführung	3320
Personal- und Ausbildungswesen	3370
Führung und Zusammenarbeit	3180
Geschäftsführung in:	
– Kleinbetrieben	3390
Das 99-Tage-Training	3440
Gepr. Kredit- und Finanzierungsfachmann	3350
Kaufmännisches Grundwissen	3150
Erfolgreich verkaufen	3190
Erfolgstraining/ Persönlichkeitsbildung	3380
Werbung und Verkauf	3420
Grafik und Design	3410

TECHNIK

Maschinenbau-Techniker	5010
Chemo-Techniker/in	5210
Elektronik-Techniker	5140
Energie-Techniker	5150
Heizungs-, Lüftungs- und Sanitär-Techniker	5410
Hochbau-Techniker	5330
Kraftfahrzeug-Techniker	5020
Kunststoff-Techniker	5220
Kaufm. Wissen für Ingenieure und Techniker	6010
Baustatik	6020
Industriemeister Elektrotechnik	6060
Industriemeister Metall	6030

NEUE Fernkurse

Existenzgründung	3570
BWL in Englisch	2222
Bilanzpraktiker	3250
Zertifikat-Kursus "London Chamber of Commerce	2221
Kraftfahrzeugtechnik	6080
Kraftfahrzeugelektronik	6090
Wirtschaftskorrespondent/in:	
- Französisch	2430
- Italienisch	2550

FERN AKADEMIE
für Erwachsenenbildung, Abt. 146 FL
Doberaner Weg 22 · 22143 Hamburg
Tel. 040 / 677 80 78 · BTX: FERNAKADEMIE #

Advertisement, "Entdecken Sie Ihren Weg zum Erfolg" from *TV Spielfilm*. Reprinted by permission of *FERNAKADEMIE Für Erwachsenenbildung, Germany*.

Copyright © by Holt, Rinehart and Winston. All rights reserved.

Realia 11-1: The REWE ad

1. **Reading/Listening** Have students read along silently as you read the REWE ad aloud. Ask students to allow you to read it through one time completely without interruption. Read it a second time, allowing interruptions for new vocabulary definitions and general questions.

2. **Thinking Critically** Now that students are completely familiar with the content of the realia, ask them why the pictures are so different. What point is the ad making? Discuss the use of double-entendre and challenge students to find other double meaning associations from their own experience. (For instance, one can speak of digesting both food and information.)

3. **Speaking (Thinking Critically)** Engage students in a discussion regarding job training. Do they think that Germany has greater requirements and higher standards? If so, why? What kind of training do Americans have to do in order to take a retail sales position? How do they think the level of general societal respect differs, if at all, for American salespeople versus German salespeople?

4. **Writing** Have students write a letter of application for a sales position as if they had graduated from this program. You may ask them to address it to a fictional retail store or a well-known establishment. Suggest they target the size of the store and the kind of products sold. Ask them to adjust their 'sales pitch' of themselves to that market. Tell them to emphasize the knowledge and skills they have learned through REWE, including convincing the personnel director or store owner of their knowledge of the products. Students can personalize this exercise by pretending to apply to a camping supply company, if camping is their particular interest, or a music distributor, if they are big music fans, etc.

Realia 11-2: The career characteristics checklist

1. **Speaking** Ask students what jobs or careers they have thought about pursuing or have already had. Ask why people generally choose certain jobs. Make a list on the chalkboard or on a transparency of the jobs or careers mentioned and the reasons for those choices.

2. **Reading** Ask each student to read the list and check those attributes of a career or job that are important to him or her. Ask them to compare the values given in the list to those given during the **Speaking** activity. If there are any that the students thought of that are not on the realia, have students list them on the realia sheet or on the chalkboard.

3. **Writing** Have students make a table with headings for each of the main attributes they wish to have in a job or career. Tell them to focus on the most important six or seven. Put key words for those attributes down the first column. Suggest students brainstorm, either independently or in pairs, about any job or career that interests them that would fulfill any one of those categories. Write those across

Copyright © by Holt, Rinehart and Winston. All rights reserved.

the top as column headers. They would then give a percentage estimating the extent to which each attribute is fulfilled in each career. For example:

	Teacher	Artist	Etc.
Creativity	70%	100%	
Independence	20%	100%	
Growth	85%	90%	
Security	100%	0%	
Income	75%	unknown	

4. **Thinking Critically** If students find two or more careers particularly appealing based on the table they created, encourage them to work with the table and determine if it is possible to synthesize careers to fulfill more of the attributes they are seeking. For example:

	Art Teacher
Creativity	85%
Independence	25%
Growth	85%
Security	100%
Income	75%

Realia 11-3: The Fernakademie ad

1. **Reading** Have students scan the text for cognates and adopted English words. Ask them then to read the text through, using context clues to guess at any unfamiliar vocabulary. As students go through the text a third time, ask them to underline or highlight aspects of the promotion that have special personal appeal.

2. **Speaking (Thinking Critically)** Ask the students to compare possible disadvantages to each of the advantages of correspondence courses suggested in this promotion.

3. **Speaking (Role-playing)** Students are to role-play a situation in which they are trying to convince their parents that distance schooling is better for them than another choice, such as attending a university. Students will also role-play the part of the parent(s).

4. **Listening** If possible, bring in guest speakers who have careers or jobs in any of the fields listed as courses in this realia. Ask the speakers to share their background, training, and the advantages and disadvantages of what they do for a living.

5. **Writing** Each student can write a letter, in the form of advice to a friend, suggesting that the **Fernakademie** would be the perfect solution to the friend's indecision about the future.

Copyright © by Holt, Rinehart and Winston. All rights reserved.

REALIA

Realia 12-1

 INFORMATION

DAS DEUTSCHE SPRACHDIPLOM

Das Deutsche Sprachdiplom ist ein offizieller Nachweis von Deutschkenntnissen. Es umfaßt 2 Stufen und wird im allgemeinen zweimal jährlich an deutschen Auslandsschulen abgenommen.

Das Bestehen der Stufe I (in der Regel am Ende des 10. Schuljahres) ermöglicht die Aufnahme in ein Studienkolleg. Hier können ausländische Studenten in einjähriger Vorbereitung die sprachliche und fachliche Hochschulreife erwerben.

Stufe 2 ist der Nachweis von Deutschkenntnissen, die offiziell zum Hochschulstudium in der Bundesrepublik erforderlich sind. Sie wird in der Regel an deutschen Auslandsschulen in der obersten Klasse abgenommen.

Auf beiden Stufen besteht das deutsche Sprachdiplom aus einer schriftlichen und einer mündlichen Prüfung. Die schriftliche Prüfung wird zentral korrigiert und bewertet. Zuständig für die Organisation ist die Zentralsstelle für das Auslandsschulwesen in Köln. Die mündliche Prüfung wird am Tag der schriftlichen Prüfung an der jeweiligen Auslandsschule abgenommen.

In jeder Ausgabe von TIP stehen je zwei Lesetexte aus dem mündlichen Prüfungsteil, die thematisch zu aktuellen JUMA-Artikeln passen (s. S. 47). Weitere Informationen zum Deutschen Sprachdiplom:

Ständige Konferenz der Kultusminister der Länder in der Bundesrepublik Deutschland (KMK)
Nassestr. 8
D-W 53113 Bonn 1

oder

Bundesverwaltungsamt
Zentralstelle für das Auslandsschulwesen
Barbarastraße 1
D-W 50735 Köln 60

Ständige Konferenz der Kultusminister der Länder in der Bundesrepublik Deutschland

DEUTSCHES SPRACHDIPLOM
Erste Stufe

Jana Mustermann

hat durch eine schriftliche und eine mündliche Prüfung in der deutschen Sprache dieses Diplom erworben.

Die Erste Stufe des Deutschen Sprachdiploms der Kultusministerkonferenz gilt als Nachweis der Deutschkenntnisse, die für die Aufnahme in ein Studienkolleg in Deutschland erforderlich sind.

Vorsitzender des Zentralen Ausschusses für das Deutsche Sprachdiplom der Kultusministerkonferenz

Leiter der für den Prüfungsort zuständigen Auslandsvertretung der Bundesrepublik Deutschland

Das Deutsche Sprachdiplom ist ein offizieller Nachweis von Deutschkenntnissen.

"Information: Das deutsche Sprachdiplom" from TIP, 2/93, April 1993, p. 13. Reprinted by permission of **Tiefdruck Schwann-Bagel GmbH**.

Copyright © by Holt, Rinehart and Winston. All rights reserved.

Kurs 1:
Zeichnen und Malen
Programm-Teilauszug
• Spielerische Strichübungen als Einführung • Formen- und Strukturlehre • Lineares Zeichnen • Perspektivlehre • Kompositionslehre (Bildaufbau) für Stilleben, Landschaften und Figuren • Farbenlehre • Behandlung aller Mal- und Zeichentechniken wie Bleistift, Kohle, Feder, Aquarell, Oel, Pastell, Gouache, Linolschnitt, Batik, Mosaik usw. • Porträtieren • Landschaftszeichnen und -malen • Aktzeichnen und -malen • Karikatur • Kunst- und Stilgeschichte • Abschlusszeugnis.

Kurs 2:
Innenarchitektur
Programm-Teilauszug
• Zeichnerische Grundausbildung • Materialkunde • Stilkunde • Perspektiv- und Konstruktionslehre • Modellbau • Möbelentwurfslehre • Gestaltung einzelner Raumelemente • Einrichtung eines Einfamilienhauses • Innenarchitektur in Hotel-, Restaurant- und Ladenbau • Technisches Baufachzeichnen • Bauentwurfslehre • Baustoffkunde • Holzbaukonstruktionen • Elektrische Hausinstallationen • Kunstgeschichte • Abschlusszeugnis.

Kurs 3:
Modezeichnen
Programm-Teilauszug
• Zeichnerische Grundausbildung • Figürliches Zeichnen • Aktzeichnen • Porträtieren • Faltenwurfübungen • Detailzeichnen von Kopfbedeckungen, Händen, Schuhen, Accessoires • Schnittmusterzeichnen • Materialkunde • Stoffberechnungen und Zuschneiden • Entwerfen von Kleidern, Hosen, Mänteln, Jupes, Blusen, Jacken • Modell-Kollektions-Entwerfen • Kostümgeschichte • Kunst- und Stilgeschichte • Werbe- und Modegrafik • Abschlusszeugnis.

Kurs 4:
Werbegrafik
Programm-Teilauszug
• Zeichnerische Grundausbildung mit Porträtieren, Akt- und Landschaftsmalen • Schriftenentwurfslehre • Typographie • Gestaltung von Inseraten, Drucksachen, Prospekten, Firmensigneten, Plakaten, Katalogen, Verpackungen, Illustrationen • Vom Layout zur Reinzeichnung • Ausstellungsgestaltung • Allgemeine Werbelehre • Werbetext • Druckverfahren • Fotografie • Papierkunde • Werbeplanung und -kontrolle • Modegrafik • Kunst- und Stilgeschichte • Abschlusszeugnis.

Neue Kunstschule Zürich
(Unter Leitung und Mitwirkung von staatl. dipl. Zeichenlehrern und Kunstpädagogen)
Räffelstrasse 11, CH-8045 Zürich   **Anrufe aus Deutschland-W: Tel. 00411/462 14 18**
Anrufe aus der Schweiz: Tel. 01/462 14 18   **Anrufe aus Deutschland-O: Tel. 06411/462 14 18**

Advertisement, "Neue Kunstschule Zürich." Reprinted by permission of *Neue Kunstschule Zürich*.

Copyright © by Holt, Rinehart and Winston. All rights reserved.

Realia 12-3

Noch so jung und schon ganz oben

Anfang Dreißig und schon Chef eines großen Hotels? Gar nicht so selten! Denn im Hotel- und Gaststättengewerbe machen junge Leute schnell Karriere. Und immer wieder sagen sie: «Für mich ist das der schönste Beruf der Welt!»

Neugierig? Dann schreiben Sie oder rufen Sie an. Die Broschüre mit authentischen Karriere-beispielen und vielen Informationen kommt kostenlos!

Erlebnis-Berufe in Hotels und Gaststätten

Koch/Köchin
Restaurantfachmann/-frau
Hotelfachmann/-frau
Hotelkaufmann/-frau
Fachgehilfe/-in

Übrigens: Nur eine erfolgreiche Ausbildung garantiert einen erfolg-reichen Berufsweg. Baden-Württemberg ist ein Musterland der Gastlichkeit! Erstklassige Aus-bildungsbetriebe zeitigen seit Jahren beste Ergebnisse.

Komm zu uns ins Team der Gastlichkeit damit die Zukunft stimmt!

COUPON:

Schicken Sie mir bitte das Karriere-Paket über die fünf Ausbildungsberufe im Hotel- und Gaststättengewerbe!

Name: _____

Straße: _____

PLZ/Ort: _____

Ausschneiden und einsenden an den Hotel- und Gaststättenverband Baden-Württemberg, Augustenstraße 6 70178 Stuttgart, Tel. 0711/61988-0 Fax 616444

Advertisement, "Noch so jung und schon ganz oben" from *Jugendherberge*. Reprinted by permission of **Hotel- und Gaststättenverband**.

Copyright © by Holt, Rinehart and Winston. All rights reserved.

REALIA

Realia 12-1: The Deutsches Sprachdiplom information

1. **Reading** Copy just the diploma (you may want to enlarge it) and give one to each student to read.

2. **Listening** In German, give students a brief overview of the article and the purpose of the diploma.

3. **Speaking** Call on students to say why a country might require a certain degree of proficiency in its official language for entrance into its institutions of higher learning. Ask them whether they think this is a good idea or not, and why.

4. **Challenge** Suggest that students call or write universities and question the language requirements for native students and for foreign students. Are they state or federally mandated? Ask them to report their findings to the class.

5. **Reading/Listening** Call on successive students to read portions of the text while the rest of the class reads along silently. If a student stumbles on a word, model it, but don't explain it. Record it on a transparency or chalkboard. At the end, return to the list and ask what each word means. If no one knows, ask for possible meanings based on context. Have students vote for the best guess. Then tell them its meaning or allow them to look it up in their dictionaries.

6. **Reading/Speaking/Writing** Tell the class that you are going to use this article to give them a mock written and oral test in language proficiency. Ask them to read the article through one more time. Afterwards, call on students randomly to answer your questions about various aspects of the content. When the oral part is completed, ask each student individually to write a summary of the article. You may wish to have partners exchange papers and correct each other's work.

Realia 12-2: The Neue Kunstschule ad

1. **Reading** Request that students scan the text for cognates and false cognates. Point out that there are many technical terms in this ad and that some of them are quite similar to English, but are not exact equivalents. Tell them to relate each term to the others in the particular course and to the pictures to derive an exact meaning for each program. Also, have them watch for certain courses which appear in all the programs.

2. **Speaking (Thinking Critically)** Ask students to compare the terms found in the realia to their English equivalents or near equivalents. You may wish to ask the gifted artists of your class, if you have any, to volunteer the most precise definitions. Ask them to say why they think certain classes appear in all the programs. Have your students pay particular attention to the seal in the upper right corner of each text box. Can your students imagine how all these courses can be given at a distance? If so, how?

3. **Writing** For fun, ask each student to choose one of the drawings to replicate. After he or she has sketched it, ask the student to evaluate it and to answer the following questions alongside the picture: 1) Which courses does he or she most

Copyright © by Holt, Rinehart and Winston. All rights reserved.

need and least need (rank them in order of importance based on the drawing); 2) Is he or she likely to pursue a career in art?

4. **Listening** Allow volunteers to show their artwork and to share their evaluations of the work with the whole class. You might also invite students with a strong art background to share some of their other work and explain it to the class in terms of the vocabulary in this realia.

Realia 12-3 Ad from the Hotel- und Gaststättenverband

1. **Writing (Thinking Critically)** Have students look at the picture without the text. Ask them what popular English idiom is being projected by this graphic (climbing the ladder of success) and tell them or ask if they know a German equivalent to that expression. Based on that phrase and the picture below the ladder, ask them to make predictions about the content of the text. Tell them to think specifically about what vocabulary they would expect to find, and since it is an ad, what promises and offers are likely to be made. After they have had some time to write some predictions, reveal the first heading and, if it stimulates some more ideas, allow them a little more time to write. Then reveal the second heading and do the same. Compile a class list of predictions, drawing from students' individual work.

2. **Reading** As students read the text, have them underline or highlight those words that match or are variations of their predictions.

3. **Listening** Reread those parts which make overt claims and promises, such as **Noch so jung und schon ganz oben** and **Für mich ist das der schönste Beruf der Welt!**

4. **Speaking** Find out, by a show of hands, how many students believe these claims. Ask how many of them had considered a career in the hotel industry prior to reading the ad and how many would give it more serious thought after reading the ad. Encourage students to share their thoughts, impressions, and reasons derived from prior experience and this ad that would make them more or less inclined to enter this field.

Copyright © by Holt, Rinehart and Winston. All rights reserved.

Situation Cards

Situation 1-1: Interview

I'm an acquaintance of yours and we meet at school the first day of fall classes. I would like to know what you did during summer vacation. How would you respond to the following questions?

Was hast du in den Ferien gemacht?

Wohin bist du gefahren?

Was hast du dort gemacht?

Situation 1-2: Interview

I just broke my leg last weekend playing rugby and you're visiting me. Since I have a lot of time on my hands, I'm now interested in everybody else's injury stories. How would you respond to the following?

Hast du dich schon mal verletzt?

Wie? Wann? Wo?

Situation (global): Interview

I'm considering a trip to a big city for my next vacation, and I'm gathering information. How would you respond to the following questions?

Hast du schon mal eine Großstadt besucht? Welche?

Was hast du dort gemacht, besucht, besichtigt?

Wie hat es dir gefallen?

SITUATION CARDS

Copyright © by Holt, Rinehart and Winston. All rights reserved.

Situation Cards: Role-playing

Situation 1-1: Role-playing

Student A   It's the first day of school and class hasn't started yet. You didn't see your partner all summer long, and you would like to know how he or she spent his or her summer. Ask your partner what he or she did, where he or she went, how long he or she stayed, etc.

Student B   It's the first day of school and class hasn't started yet. You and your partner didn't see each other all summer long, and you would like to tell him or her about your vacation and also find out how he or she spent his or her summer. First answer your partner's questions, then ask him or her the same questions.

Situation 1-2: Role-playing

Student A   You broke your foot over the weekend and are lying on the couch at home with a new cast on. Your partner has come over and is curious about your accident. Answer his or her questions, and then ask your partner if he or she has ever had an injury. If so, ask how it happened.

Student B   You are at the house of your partner who broke his or her leg over the weekend. Ask how it happened and if it still hurts. Express sympathy. Answer your partner's questions about any injuries you or someone else may have had in the past.

Situation (global): Role-playing

Student A   You visited Dresden, Hamburg, Frankfurt and Berlin this summer. Your partner is considering a trip to a large city in Germany. Answer questions about the cities you visited, and suggest which city he or she ought to visit.

Student B   Your partner visited several cities in Germany this summer. Ask where your partner went, what he or she did there, where he or she stayed, and how he or she liked it. Ask your partner to recommend the city he or she enjoyed most.

SITUATION CARDS

Komm mit! Level 3, Chapter 1

Copyright © by Holt, Rinehart and Winston. All rights reserved.

Name _____ Klasse _____ Datum _____

Situation 2-1: Interview

We get together at a café because you're planning a trip to Germany and I'm interested in knowing why you want to visit the following cities. How would you respond to these questions?

Warum willst du nach Berlin fahren?

Warum willst du nach Dresden fahren?

Warum willst du nach Weimar fahren?

Situation 2-2: Interview

Both of us are interested in international travel and are imagining that we have unlimited cash flow and can go anywhere we want. Respond to the following questions.

Möchtest du mal reisen?

Wenn ja, wohin? Warum?

Wenn nein, warum nicht?

Was weißt du schon über diese Stadt? (über diesen Ort?)

Situation (global): Interview

I would like to go on a trip in Germany and visit some cities, and, since you know a lot about Germany, I'd like some suggestions from you. How would you respond to the following questions?

Welche Gegenden sind schön?

Welche Städte soll ich besuchen?

Warum? Was gibt's da zu sehen?

SITUATION CARDS

Copyright © by Holt, Rinehart and Winston. All rights reserved.

Situation Cards: Role-playing

Situation 2-1: Role-playing

Student A   You and your partner are planning a trip somewhere. You have reservations about all the places he or she suggests visiting. Think of some reasons to tell your partner why you don't want to visit the places he or she suggests. Suggest some other places and try to work out a compromise for a place to visit.

Student B   You and your partner are planning a trip somewhere. Your partner seems to have reservations about all the places you suggest. Listen to his or her reasons, then suggest some other places the two of you might visit.

Situation 2-2: Role-playing

Student A   You and your partner have just won a prize from a travel agency and can spend one week traveling in Germany, but you must travel together. Where would you like to go? Why? Does your partner agree? Decide together where you will go and what you will do there.

Student B   You and your partner have just won a prize from a travel agency, and can spend one week traveling in Germany, but you must travel together. Where would you like to go? Why? Does your partner agree? Decide together where you will go and what you will do there.

Situation (global): Role-playing

Student A   You spent last summer in the German-speaking countries and visited many different cities and parts of the countryside. Answer your partner's questions about your trip.

Student B   You are going to spend two or three weeks in the German-speaking countries this summer. Your partner was there last summer. Find out where he or she went and ask for suggestions for places you should visit. Ask your partner why you should visit the places he or she suggests.

Copyright © by Holt, Rinehart and Winston. All rights reserved.

SITUATION CARDS

Situation 3-1: Interview

I would like to know what you think about various subjects having to do with personal appearance. How would you respond to the following questions?

Was hältst du von Mode?

Ist es wichtig, Biokost zu essen?

Was hältst du von Bodybuilding?

Ist es wichtig, sich gut zu ernähren? Warum?

Situation 3-2: Interview

I'm a new friend and I would like to know how you deal with the stresses and pressures of life in high school. How would you respond to the following questions?

Bist du manchmal down? Warum?

Was machst du, wenn es dir schlecht geht?

Was rätst du mir, wenn ich zu dick werde? Wenn ich mich nicht fit halte? Wenn ich immer müde bin?

Situation (global): Interview

I'm your best friend, and we're discussing the ideal boyfriend or girlfriend. How would you respond to the following questions?

Der ideale Partner oder die ideale Partnerin:

Macht er oder sie viel Sport?

Muss er oder sie fit sein?

Wie wichtig ist für ihn oder für sie das Aussehen? Klamotten? Haare?

Wie wichtig ist Mode für ihn oder für sie?

Was für eine Lebenseinstellung (positiv/optimistisch/pessimistisch) hat er oder sie? Ist es wichtig, daß zwei Leute, die sich mögen, ähnliche Lebenseinstellungen haben?

SITUATION CARDS

Copyright © by Holt, Rinehart and Winston. All rights reserved.

Name _____ Klasse _____ Datum _____

 Situation Cards: Role-playing

Situation 3-1: Role-playing

Student A   You are eating lunch with **Student B** and the discussion has turned to issues of health and appearance. Ask **Student B** what his or her opinion is about the importance of fashion, eating right, exercising, bodybuilding, etc.

Student B   You are eating lunch with **Student A**. Answer **Student A**'s questions by giving your opinions about the issues he or she asks you about. Then ask **Student A** if he or she agrees with you, or whether he or she has different opinions.

Situation 3-2: Role-playing

Student A   Your friend, **Student B**, appears to be unhappy. Ask him or her what the matter is and why. Then ask **Student B** what he or she usually does to get rid of a bad mood. If you can think of any other suggestions, make them.

Student B   You are in a bad mood. Tell your friend, **Student A**, what's bothering you and how you plan to cheer yourself up. Ask your partner if he or she has any other suggestions.

Situation (global): Role-playing

Student A   You are at a party and you just saw the boy or girl of your dreams. Tell your friend, **Student B**, what this dream person looks like, then answer your partner's questions about dream persons in general. Find out **Student B**'s opinions, too.

Student B   You and your friend, **Student A**, are attending a party. **Student A** excitedly describes to you a person who has just arrived—it's the person **Student A** has waited all of his or her life to meet! After listening to the description and responding appropriately, discuss with **Student A** what is important in a partner.

Komm mit! Level 3, Chapter 3

Copyright © by Holt, Rinehart and Winston. All rights reserved.

Situation Cards: Interview

Situation 4-1: Interview

I'm interested in your relationship with your family. How do you respond to the following question?

Hast du Geschwister?

Wie viele?

Wie ist dein Verhältnis zu deinen Geschwistern?

Zu deinen Eltern?

Gibt es manchmal zu Hause Krach?

Worüber?

Situation 4-2: Interview

I'm a sociologist and I'm doing a study about prejudice in the German schools. How do you react (honestly) to these questions?

Hast du Vorurteile gegen andere Leute?

Kennst du Leute, die Vorurteile haben?

Welche?

Warum haben sie Vorurteile?

Wie kannst du oder wie kann man seine Vorurteile abschaffen?

Situation (global): Interview

You were born in Germany, but your parents were born in Turkey. I'm your teacher and I notice you seem to be having trouble at school, especially with your peers. How do you react to the following questions?

Wie fühlst du dich hier in der Schule?

Gibt es zu Hause Probleme?

Meinst du, dass die anderen Schüler Vorurteile gegen dich haben? Welche?

Was könnten wir — du, ich, die anderen Schüler und deine Eltern — machen, um die Situation zu verbessern?

SITUATION CARDS

Copyright © by Holt, Rinehart and Winston. All rights reserved.

Situation Cards: Role-playing

Situation 4-1: Role-playing

Student A You just had an argument with your parents about something at home and your partner is concerned. Answer his or her questions about the argument. Ask your partner what his relationship with his parents is like, and if he or she has similar problems at home.

Student B Your partner just had an argument with his or her parents. Ask him or her what happened, what they argued about. Give him or her any suggestions or advice that comes to mind. Answer your partner's questions about your relationship with your parents.

Situation 4-2: Role-playing

Student A You are an American exchange student in Germany, and you notice that the Turkish teenagers in your class don't seem to interact with the Germans much. Ask your partner (a German) whether there is a lot of prejudice against **Ausländer** in the school, and if so, why. Answer your partner's questions.

Student B Your partner, an American exhange student, wants to know what the situation is with regard to **Ausländer** at your Gymnasium. Answer his or her questions and ask about the situation in the United States; are there prejudices, against whom, and why?

Situation (global): Role-playing

Student A Your school is having a special study group for German students and **Ausländer** to discuss their similarities and differences. You are a German student and your partner is a Turkish student. Discuss the question: **Wollen, können, sollen die Türken sich besser in die deutsche Gesellschaft integrieren?**

Student B Play the role of a Turkish student in a study group discussing similarities and differences between Germans and **Ausländer**. Respond to your partner's questions and ask: **Was können deutsche Schüler tun, um türkische Schüler besser zu verstehen?**

Copyright © by Holt, Rinehart and Winston. All rights reserved.

SITUATION CARDS

Situation Cards: Interviews

Situation 5-1: Interview

I'm a new friend and we are getting to know each other better —
talking about things we wanted to do when we were younger but
didn't do, about things we would do if ..., etc. How do you
respond to the following questions?

Was könntest du machen, wenn du schon 18 wärst?

**Was hättest du gern gemacht, als du 12 warst, und warum
hast du es nicht gemacht?**

**Was könntest du jetzt machen, machst es aber nicht?
Warum machst du das nicht?**

Situation 5-2: Interview

I'm from Germany and I'm interested in knowing if children in
the United States have the same kinds of restraints and rules that
German children have. How do you respond to the following
questions?

Was durftest du nicht tun, als du 12 warst?

Kannst du das jetzt tun?

Was durfte man früher tun, was man jetzt nicht tun darf?

Was durfte man früher nicht tun, was man jetzt tun kann?

Situation (global): Interview

I want to play tennis with you, but you can't just now. How do
you respond to the following questions?

**Warum kannst du mit mir nicht Tennis spielen? Was machst
du jetzt?**

Glaubst du, dass man früher mehr Zeit hatte?

**Was meinst du, wie das Leben vor 50 Jahren anders war als
heute?**

SITUATION CARDS

Copyright © by Holt, Rinehart and Winston. All rights reserved.

Situation Cards: Role-playing

Situation 5-1: Role-playing

Student A   Your partner is a new friend, and the two of you are getting to know each other better. Right now you are talking about your dreams and frustrations. Ask your partner what he or she would be doing if he or she were 18. Ask what he or she would have liked to do but couldn't at the age of 12. Ask what he or she can't do now, and why not. Answer your partner's questions.

Student B   You and your partner have recently become friends and are getting to know each other better. Right now you're talking about your dreams and frustrations. First answer your partner's questions, and then ask your partner the same questions.

Situation 5-2: Role-playing

Student A   As a German exchange student, you are interested in your partner's personal history and the history of Americans in general. Ask what kinds of restrictions he or she had at the age of 12, and whether he or she can do those things now. Ask how life was different for his or her grandparents.

Student B   Your German friend is asking you questions about how things were for you when you were younger, compared to now, and about how it was for Americans in general a generation or two ago. Answer your partner's questions, and then ask in what ways that is similar or different from life in Germany.

Situation (global): Role-playing

Student A   Your partner calls to ask if you can play tennis in half an hour. Say that you can't and what you have to do instead. Your partner wants to know if you think people of previous generations had as little time as your generation. Tell your partner your opinion, and ask for his or hers.

Student B   Ask your partner if he or she can meet you to play tennis in half an hour. Tell your partner you're sorry he or she is so busy, then ask your partner if he or she thinks people of previous generations also had so little time on their hands. Give your opinion on this question.

Copyright © by Holt, Rinehart and Winston. All rights reserved.

Situation 6-1: Interview

I'm interested in your attitude toward the media. How do you answer the following questions?

Welche Medien nutzt du? Warum?

Glaubst du, dass ein Medium besser ist als ein anderes? Welches?

Fernsehen macht dumm. Nimm dazu Stellung, und begründe deine Antwort!

Situation 6-2: Interview

I'm a German exchange student with a somewhat arrogant attitude. Defend yourself and your country against the following allegations.

Unsere Zeitungen sind besser als eure.

Unsere Radiosendungen sind interessanter als eure.

Unsere Kinder sehen nicht so viel fern wie eure.

Situation (global): Interview

I want to know what you think about television. How do you respond to the following questions?

Was hältst du vom Fernsehen?

Inwiefern (*to what extent*) ist Fernsehen nützlich, und inwiefern ist Fernsehen schädlich?

Du siehst drei bis vier Stunden am Abend Fernsehen. Begründe das!

Du siehst selten fern—vielleicht zwei Stunden in der Woche. Begründe es!

SITUATION CARDS

Copyright © by Holt, Rinehart and Winston. All rights reserved.

Situation Cards: Role-playing

Situation 6-1: Role-playing

Student A   You are doing a study for your sociology class about media. Ask your partner which media he or she makes the most use of and why. You would like to know if he finds one medium better than another. And you want to get his or her reaction to the statement: **Fernsehen macht dumm.**

Student B   Your partner is interviewing you about media for a project for his or her sociology class. Answer his or her questions. You are curious about your partner's opinions on the same questions, so ask what he or she thinks.

Situation 6-2: Role-playing

Student A   You are at a party with a most obnoxious exchange student, who claims that everything in his or her country is better than things in your country. Respond to this student's assertions that various things are better in his or her country.

Student B   You are an exchange student, and, based on your observations and experience, you feel that almost everything in your country is better, more interesting, etc. than it is here. Tell your partner how you feel about the television, radio, newspapers, children's behavior, teachers, schools, etc. in your country and in the U.S.A.

Situation (global): Role-playing

Student A   You and your friend are sitting around with nothing to do. Suggest watching television, and then discuss your attitudes toward television with your partner.

Student B   You and your friend are sitting around with nothing to do. Your partner suggests watching television, but you think television is harmful. Ask your partner what he or she thinks, and then discuss the pros and cons of television together.

SITUATION CARDS

Copyright © by Holt, Rinehart and Winston. All rights reserved.

Name _____ Klasse _____ Datum _____

Situation 7-1: Interview

In Germany the television advertising system is different from the American system: german television airs commercials in two blocks of ten minutes each and no advertisements during the programs. What is your opinion on the following questions?

Welches System ist besser für die Zuschauer? Das deutsche oder das amerikanische? Warum?

Welches System ist besser für die Geschäftsleute, die viel Geld für Fernsehreklame ausgeben: das deutsche oder das amerikanische? Warum?

Situation 7-2: Interview

I'm a German exchange student and I'm fascinated by television advertising in the United States. I want to know how you react to it. Please answer the following questions.

Welche Werbungen findest du am effektivsten? Warum?

Welche Werbungen nerven dich am meisten? Warum?

Welche Werbung findest du am dümmsten? Warum?

Welche Werbung gefällt dir am besten? Warum?

Situation (global): Interview

I'm going to make some statements and I'd like you to take a position and support it.

In den meisten Werbungen erfährt man nichts über die Produkte.

Werbung ist teuer und nützt sowieso nichts.

Frauen werden in der Werbung meistens nur in stereotypischen Rollen dargestellt.

Kinder werden in der Werbung ausgenutzt (*exploited*).

SITUATION CARDS

Copyright © by Holt, Rinehart and Winston. All rights reserved.

Situation Cards: Role-playing

Situation 7-1: Role-playing

Student A   You are from Germany, and you think the American television advertising system is better, because it is more effective for the advertisers and because the viewer has a break from watching TV. Your partner has a different opinion. Discuss your opinions.

Student B   You are from the United States, and you think the German television advertising system is better, because the viewer doesn't have to sit through commercials during a program and because you think it's less effective for the advertisers, which you think is good, because you find television advertising manipulative. Discuss your opinion with your partner.

Situation 7-2: Role-playing

Student A   You're at a party, and you're discussing television ads with your partner. Ask him or her which specific ads he or she likes the most; the least. Ask which ones he or she finds most effective and least effective and why.

Student B   You're at a party and you're discussing television ads with your partner. First respond to your partner's questions, then ask him or her which specific ads he or she likes the most and which the least. Find out which ones he or she finds most effective and which least effective. Ask him or her why.

Situation (global): Role-playing

Student A   You don't exactly like television advertising. Tell your partner how you think it is ineffective (or too effective) and what you think the problems with it are. Support your opinions and ask your partner for his or her opinions.

Student B   Your partner is telling you what he or she doesn't like about television advertising. Express your opinion about his or her statements, and then say why you have that opinion.

SITUATION CARDS

Copyright © by Holt, Rinehart and Winston. All rights reserved.

Situation 8-1: Interview

You are a German student spending a year at an American high school. I am a friend of your host family's and I'm curious about your experiences here. How do you respond to the following questions?

Was hat dich bei den Amerikanern überrascht?

Was hat dich enttäuscht?

Was stört dich? Was regt dich auf?

Situation 8-2: Interview

You are an American student spending a year at a **Gymnasium** in Germany. I am a friend of your host family's and I'm curious about your experiences here. How do you respond to the following questions?

Wie hast du die Deutschen früher gesehen? Welche Klischees oder Vorurteile hattest du?

Wie hat sich deine Meinung geändert? Wie siehst du die Deutschen jetzt?

Situation (global): Interview

I am a German about to go to the United States for one year. How do you answer the following questions to help me prepare to experience American culture?

Kannst du mir einige Tips geben?

Was für Warnungen würdest du mir geben?

Was empfiehlst du mir?

SITUATION CARDS

Copyright © by Holt, Rinehart and Winston. All rights reserved.

Name _____ Klasse _____ Datum _____

 Situation Cards: Role-playing

Situation 8-1: Role-playing

Student A You were in Germany for one year and are at a gathering of Americans and Germans on their way home from a year as exchange students. Your partner, a German, was in the United States. Ask what about Americans surprised, disappointed, annoyed or displeased him or her.

Student B You are a German student who has been in the United States for one year and are at a gathering of American and German students on their way home from a year as exchange students. Your partner, an American, was in Germany. Ask what about Germans surprised, disappointed, annoyed or displeased him or her.

Situation 8-2: Role-playing

Student A You were in Germany for one year and are at a gathering of exchange students. Your partner, a German, was in the United States. Ask what assumptions he or she had about Americans before going there, and how they have changed.

Student B You are a German student who has been in the United States for one year and are at a gathering of Americans and Germans on their way home from a year as exchange students. Your partner, an American, was in Germany. Ask what assumptions he or she had about Germans before going there, and how they have changed.

Situation (global): Role-playing

Student A You are an American exchange student in Germany, and your partner has just found out that he or she will be an exchange student in the United States next year. Answer his or her questions.

Student B You are a German student and you have just found out that you will be an exchange student in the United States next year. Ask your partner, an American exchange student, what tips he or she can give you. Does he or she have any suggestions or warnings?

SITUATION CARDS

Komm mit! Level 3, Chapter 8

Copyright © by Holt, Rinehart and Winston. All rights reserved.

Situation 9-1: Interview

I am conducting a survey about attitudes toward environmental issues. How would you respond to the following questions?

Welche Umweltsorgen hast du?

Wer ist an den Umweltproblemen schuld?

Was soll gemacht werden, um die Probleme zu lösen?

Was würdest du sagen, wenn im Park jemand eine Flasche wegwirft?

Situation 9-2: Interview

Your little sibling's best friend is doing some research for his social studies class on household approaches to environmental protection. How would you respond to these questions he or she asks you?

Was wird bei dir für die Umwelt gemacht? Warum?

Was könnte oder sollte für die Umwelt alles gemacht werden?

Situation (global): Interview

You and I are sitting around dreaming about an environmentally friendly government. How would you respond to the following questions?

Was für Gesetze sollte es geben?

Was würdest du machen, wenn du Kanzler wärst?

SITUATION CARDS

Copyright © by Holt, Rinehart and Winston. All rights reserved.

Situation Cards: Role-playing

Situation 9-1: Role-playing

Student A   You are in a park and you see someone (your partner) throw a bottle in the trash. How do you react? What do you say to him or her? How can you politely request that he or she improve his or her behavior?

Student B   You have just tossed a bottle in the trash in the park, when someone comes up to you and confronts you about your action. Defend your action, then ask your partner for more suggestions about recycling and other environmental practices.

Situation 9-2: Role-playing

Student A   You and your friend are discussing environmental issues. Ask your partner what he or she worries about the most, what he or she does at home in order to protect the environment, and what he or she thinks can, should, and must be done on behalf of the environment.

Student B   You and your friend are discussing environmental issues. Ask your partner what he or she worries about the most, what he or she does at home in order to protect the environment, and what he or she thinks can, should, and must be done on behalf of the environment.

Situation (global): Role-playing

Student A   You and your friend are imagining the world of tomorrow. Discuss what environmental protection laws you would like to put in place if you were a member of the government.

Student B   You and your friend are imagining the world of tomorrow. Discuss what environmental protection laws you would like to put in place if you were a member of the government.

SITUATION CARDS

Komm mit! Level 3, Chapter 9

Copyright © by Holt, Rinehart and Winston. All rights reserved.

Situation 10-1: Interview

I'm from Germany and I'm trying to learn more about American high school students' interest in cultural events. How would you respond to the following questions?

Was würdest du tun, wenn du mehr Zeit und Geld für kulturelle Interessen hättest?

Welche Persönlichkeiten der kulturellen Welt bewunderst du? Welche beneidest du? Warum?

Situation 10-2: Interview

You really love opera and you don't have enough money to go see Wagner's „Das Rheingold". How would you answer the following questions?

Worüber bist du traurig? Warum?

Wofür interessierst du dich noch?

Situation (global): Interview

I've never been to an opera before, and you just went last night. How would you respond to the following questions?

Was wurde vor der Vorstellung gemacht?

Was geschieht alles während der Oper?

Was ist nach der Vorstellung geschehen?

SITUATION CARDS

Copyright © by Holt, Rinehart and Winston. All rights reserved.

Situation Cards: Role-playing

Situation 10-1: Role-playing

Student A As a German exchange student you want to know more about American students' interest in cultural events. Ask your partner what cultural interests he has, what he would do with more time and money, and what cultural figures he admires or envies and why.

Student B You are talking to a German exchange student and you would like to know more about her interest in cultural events. Ask your partner what cultural interests she has, what she would do if she had more time and money, and what cultural figures she admires or envies and why.

Situation 10-2: Role-playing

Student A You are happy because you went to the opera last night and it was really great. Answer your friend's questions.

Student B You are really sad because you didn't have enough money to go to the opera last night. Tell your friend why you are sad, and ask him or her how the opera was.

Situation (global): Role-playing

Student A You have never been to a theater before. Ask your partner what it was like and what happened when he went last night.

Student B Your friend has never been to the theater before, but you saw Goethe's *Faust* (or another play) last night. Answer your partner's question, telling her every detail, from buying your ticket to applauding at the end of the concert.

SITUATION CARDS

Komm mit! Level 3, Chapter 10

Copyright © by Holt, Rinehart and Winston. All rights reserved.

Situation Cards: Interviews

Situation 11-1: Interview

You are at an interview with the dean of a prospective college. How would you respond to the following questions?

Was sind Ihre Pläne für die Zukunft?

Was ist schon entschieden, was noch nicht?

Situation 11-2: Interview

I am writing an article for the local newspaper about the values and dreams of today's high school students. How would you respond to the following questions?

Was gäbe es in deiner Zukunftswelt?

Worauf legst du großen Wert?

Was wirst du mit dreißig schon alles getan haben?

Situation (global): Interview

We are fellow graduates at a graduation party and I'm interested in your future. What are your responses to the following questions?

Was steht bei dir fest?

Worüber bist du froh?

Was sind deine Wünsche für die Zukunft?

SITUATION CARDS

Copyright © by Holt, Rinehart and Winston. All rights reserved.

Situation Cards: Role-playing

Situation 11-1: Role-playing

Student A   You and your partner are discussing your plans for the future. Ask your partner what he or she plans to do, which of his or her plans are decided, and which he or she is undecided about. Answer your partner's questions.

Student B   You and your partner are discussing your plans for the future. Ask your partner what he or she plans to do, which of his or her plans are decided, and which he or she is undecided about. Answer your partner's questions.

Situation 11-2: Role-playing

Student A   You and your partner are discussing your values and your thoughts about the future. Ask your partner what is important to him or her and why. Ask what he or she thinks the future might be like. Answer your partner's questions.

Student B   You and your partner are discussing your values and your thoughts about the future. Ask your partner what is important to him or her and why. Ask what he or she thinks the future might be like. Answer your partner's questions.

Situation (global): Role-playing

Student A   You and your partner just graduated and you're at a party discussing your futures. Ask your partner which plans are already certain and which are not. Ask what gives him or her a sense of relief and what he or she hopes to have accomplished by age thirty.

Student B   You and your partner just graduated and you're at a party discussing your futures. Ask your partner which plans are already certain and which are not. Ask what gives him or her a sense of relief and what he or she hopes to have accomplished by age thirty.

SITUATION CARDS

Copyright © by Holt, Rinehart and Winston. All rights reserved.

Situation Cards: Interviews

Situation 12-1: Interview

I'm upset and I need your help. How would you react to the following?

Ich habe keine tollen Klamotten. Was soll ich tun?

Meine Noten sind schlecht. Was soll ich meinen Eltern sagen?

Ich fühle mich nicht wohl.

Situation 12-2: Interview

I'm interested in your immediate plans for the future. How would you respond to the following?

Was hast du für die Zukunft geplant? Was machst du im Sommer?

Welche Pläne stehen schon fest? Welche sind noch offen?

Situation (global): Interview

I'm interested in your opinion about the future. How would you respond to the following?

Was ist dir wichtig? Was ist dir weniger wichtig?

Wie stellst du dir eine Zukunft vor, in der dir wichtige Sachen eine Rolle spielen?

SITUATION CARDS

Copyright © by Holt, Rinehart and Winston. All rights reserved.

Situation Cards: Role-playing

Situation 12-1: Role-playing

Student A   Find out what your partner is upset about, and find out how this situation came about. Express your surprise or disappointment. Give advice and say why your friend should do as you suggest.

Student B   Everything is going wrong. Answer your friend's questions about your problems and ask for advice. React to his or her advice and when you hear something that sounds logical, agree with your partner.

Situation 12-2: Role-playing

Student A   Ask your partner what his or her plans for the future are. Challenge the validity of the plans and suggest other plans.

Student B   Answer your partner's questions about your future plans. Defend your plans and say why, or admit that you're not sure and ask for suggestions or advice.

Situation (global): Role-playing

Student A   Ask your partner what is important and why. Have him or her hypothesize a future life based on those important things.

Student B   Ask your partner what is important and why. Have him or her hypothesize a future life based on those important things.

SITUATION CARDS

Copyright © by Holt, Rinehart and Winston. All rights reserved.